The Mindset They Never Taught You

The Life Lessons School, Family & Society Never Taught You.

Khushboo Sharma

This book is a work of non-fiction. The experiences, examples, and views expressed are based on personal perspectives and observations. Any resemblance to actual persons or events is coincidental.

DEDICATION

To my little boys, Nivaan and Kabir.
May these words guide you when the world feels loud and remind you of the strength already within you.

Table of Contents

Preface

My previous book, 101 Quotes They Don't Want You to Read—Break the Illusion and Build Yourself Stronger, was thought-provoking. It was a collection of 101 quotes born from my experiences and observations, and it did create a buzz.

But this book is different. I hold this book in high regard. Living in India, I realized that life here felt different from that in other parts of the world. Yet there is one universal truth: the emotions we experience while trying to understand life, purpose, and ourselves are the same everywhere. It doesn't matter where you come from or which generation you belong to—everyone passes through that confusing, exciting, overwhelming period of life. But nobody really talks about it. People see the success, not the process.

In these pages, I explore and guide you through that process.

Life in your growing years will be both enjoyable and challenging. You'll face moments of deep emotion, but also moments of laughter and fun. You'll have opportunities to explore friendships, passions, and dreams—but all of it takes time, patience, and choices.

What many people overlook is that your prime years are not solely meant for leisure. They are your foundation years. These are the years that will either directly or indirectly shape the rest of your life. The decisions you make now—in money, habits, relationships, and mindset—will either build you or break you in your later years and beyond.

This book is my attempt to convey what no one else did. It serves as a reminder to be wise, stay in control, create balance, and never underestimate the power of the most formative and insightful years of your life.

It guides you, helps you overcome your fears and doubts, and gives you the courage to make bold, outstanding decisions that can define your life.

INTRODUCTION — THE FANTASY DECADE MYTH

What is life without dreams, passion, imagination, and desire? It all looks so appealing when we're young and messy. You meet people sharing ideas, planning futures, and chasing passions; some are even living their dreams already.

But reality does not always unfold the way we expect.

. Dreams break.

. Friendships change.

. Plans collapse.

And that's why I am here: to break the biggest myth of your young and wild years, a myth every generation before you have learned the hard way.

. Ask your parents.

. Ask your mentors.

. They'll tell you the same thing.

When Life Punches You in the Face

When you first step into adulthood, you carry self-doubt, poor habits, social media pressure, and endless comparison. Life remains unpredictable, even after you've worked hard, been sincere, and done everything "right." Social media makes your situation worse. Every scroll exposes you to people who look happier, richer, or more successful. Some feel inspired; others become envious. Many destroy themselves silently through comparison. But the hardest punch is rejection, especially in love.

When you fall deeply for someone, you believe they're "the one." You attach, sometimes too intensely. Maybe the relationship lasts; maybe it doesn't. If it doesn't, it feels like your world has collapsed. You withdraw into silence. Days and nights blur. Some even become self-destructive.

Let me tell you something

This happens to everyone. Whether you are practical, emotional, tough, or naive, rejection is universal. At some point, reality will strike, and when it does, remember this: Broken dreams, failed love, and lost opportunities are not the end. They are simply parts of life. Just as you welcome joy and love, you must learn to accept loss and failure.

Balance is the key

And occasionally, life delivers its deepest blow, the loss of a loved one. That kind of loss alters you forever. It matures you emotionally; sometimes it makes you bitter

Building a Strong Foundation

Your 20s are your foundation years. How strong or fragile this foundation is will shape your 30s, 40s, and beyond. Life has no fixed blueprint. It will always be unpredictable. But some things remain equal for everyone: We all have 24 hours in a day. Emotions—we all feel them, even if differently.

So, if you believe in "YOLO," hear me out:

. Express when you're overwhelmed.

. Express when you're hurting.

. Express when you're in love.

When you open your heart, beautiful things happen. But never forget: You are the person who remains with you until the end. One day, in your 50s, you will look at your old photographs and witness multiple versions of yourself—physically, mentally, and emotionally. And yet, it will still be you.

So:

- Don't lose yourself in love.
- Don't lose hope in rejection.
- Don't give up when dreams fail.

My Lessons

. I've been there.

. I've wept until I fell asleep.

. I've been rejected in love.

. I walked away from my dream job.

. I let go of passions I once thought defined me.

And yet, I survived. That's what you must do too. Activate survival mode when needed. Be your own cheerleader. Don't wait for others to lift you. Above all, be realistic. You can love foolishly, but don't be foolish in love. You can follow passion recklessly, but don't chase illusions. When nothing makes sense, trust your instincts. They will rescue you.

Why Purpose Matters

Amid all the ups and downs, one thing keeps you grounded: Purpose. Your work and your purpose are not always the same. Work is what you do. Purpose is why you were born. Not everyone finds it. Not everyone is able to live it. But when you do, you feel an inner ease. You stop caring about what others think. Most people discover their purpose late in life, but the foundation for it begins early—often in your confused, curious, chaotic 20s. Even if your current job feels meaningless, don't panic. Keep seeking. Occasionally you receive what you ask for. Occasionally you receive what you deserve instead. Both shape you.

The Real Script of Life

When you're young, the world tells you how life "should" look: Dream job, Perfect partner, Marriage, Kids, Retirement That was the script generations before you followed. But today, people want individuality first.

Life no longer follows a linear path.

- Some will tick every box.
- Some will tick none.

. Some will feel completely alone.

. Some will discover happiness in just two.

. Some will want children but can't.

. Some will face an unplanned baby.

. Some, after all the chaos, will choose peace over everything else.

That is life—messy, unpredictable, beautiful, unfair, and breathtaking. Everyone will walk through it differently.

A Note to You

This message is for whoever is reading this.

Life is beautiful, but only if you choose to see it clearly. Every moment, every struggle, is shaping you into who you're meant to become.

. Don't accept everything they say as truth.

. Don't believe everything you see.

. Don't fall for everything you hear.

. Don't chase perfection.

But believe this: yourself. You were born for a reason. And right now, even if it feels messy, uncertain, or unfair, you are precisely where you need to be.

With you on this journey

Khushboo Sharma

Part I
FOUNDATIONS & MINDSET...

The Foundation We Come From

"You are what you come from.
Every answer that you seek lies there."

In my view, family represents the most significant aspect of our lives. In your early years, you might not realize it, but once the internal turmoil subsides, your flashbacks and memories become the primary source of discomfort in your 30s and throughout the rest of your life. Ever wonder why humans emphasize making memories? It's because as we age and slow down, we tend to step back and reflect.

That's when self-awareness grows. Sit with your parents or older friends and see that most of their talks are about their lives and experiences. What are the most frequently discussed chapters in their lives?

They always talk about their friends and family. When I was growing up, life was simple. We rarely hear about divorces, parenting issues, or toxicity. Life was about family, friends, and enjoyment. We were mostly outdoors. Mothers stayed home to care for us, and fathers were the primary breadwinners.

Almost anywhere in the world, you will discover that people lived in much simpler times. I'm not saying everyone was content, but life was less complicated then. Lately, things have changed. Families are more divided. There are various reasons for it: inflation, self-awareness, and modernization.

The dynamic of the family has changed. Many children grow up in nuclear homes, some under the care of single mothers, some under the guidance of gay parents, and some still rooted in traditional practices. With time, modernity has brought opinions, awareness, and shifting priorities. The demands on parents' attention are immense. And often, it isn't just the parents raising the child. Outsiders such as daycares, nannies, and extended families also play a major role. They shape the next generation in ways we don't even realize.

If I share my personal experience, I would say I came from a less complicated and healthier environment. We were bonded, and I grew up seeing my parents' put emotions and humanity at the center of everything. Naturally, I followed the same path. What I've observed in life is that when you come from a healthy background, you tend to empathize with people who come from a traumatic one.

You try to understand them, you forgive their outbursts, and occasionally, you even tolerate behaviors you shouldn't—because you believe they had a difficult life. But over time, you realize something important: no matter how much love or patience you demonstrate, if the other person isn't ready to face their pain, they will keep passing it on to you.

It's not enough to just feel sorry for someone's past. What really matters is whether they are willing to break the pattern and identify a solution or if they continue to blame you and the world while keeping their trauma alive. Have the courage to change the present. A person's history doesn't define their future. Their choices do.

The Invisible Influence of Family

Many of us grew up in an environment that provided for us. Its impact, whether positive or negative, becomes clear only when we step into the real world. If you come from a healthy, supportive home, your perception is clearer, and your sense of acceptance wider. You celebrate people, places, and time. But if your upbringing involved constant struggle—financial crises, unhealthy relationships, or fear—you may grow up feeling frustrated, insecure, or hesitant to trust yourself or others. Family shapes us, but as we start exploring life independently, we learn to set our own terms, to recognize what is black and what is white.

The Cycles We Repeat

Occasionally, it's not just beliefs we inherit. It's the behaviours we adopt. Take Jay, for example. He grew up watching his father physically, emotionally, and psychologically abuse his mother. His father drank constantly. Jay absorbed that behaviour without realizing it. By his teens, he was drinking casually.

Every relationship he entered failed because he repeated what he saw and didn't know how to succeed. It took years for Jay to confront himself, and it wasn't until one serious breakup nearly shattered him that he began to do so. The night he poured his drink down the sink, his hands trembled more than ever.

That was the start. It wasn't a sudden break but a gradual journey. He got help. became sober, and learned that love isn't just about what you've seen. It's about what you choose to create.

Jay's story isn't rare. Many of us imitate what we see, not what we want. Some communicate poorly in love because they have never seen healthy communication. Some suppress emotions because they were never allowed to express them. Some chase validation because they were only loved conditionally.

The Family You Never Chose

We never choose our family. It is given to us through destiny, karma, or some unseen bond, and we have to live with it. Some of us grew up with mothers who were over-possessive or indifferent. Some had fathers who were abusive, alcoholic, or overprotective. These personalities shape us and influence future relationships.

If you were raised in a family with protective parents who allowed you to be yourself, express yourself, and ensured equal respect among siblings, you naturally grow up adopting those habits. And when you see behaviours that destroy relationships, like yelling or abuse, they'll feel alien to you. You won't even entertain people who behave that way. A trustworthy family bond fosters a secure, joyful mind. An abusive or neglectful one creates doubt, insecurity, and patterns that echo in adult relationships.

Some of Us...

. Some of us were silenced before we could question.

. Some had busy parents working day and night, losing money on bills, and neglecting communication.

. Some grew up with parents who once loved each other but now only tolerated each other for the children.

. Some of us had fathers who struggled financially, endured taunts from relatives, and faced social disdain.

This led us to associate money with value, disregarding love, empathy, and peace. Some girls, especially sensitive ones, observed that their brothers were treated better, while their voices were dismissed and their opinions ignored.

They were asked to compromise rather than lead. Over time, such experiences created deep wounds—a belief that she cannot trust men, that her voice doesn't matter, and that her dreams are optional. She may rebel, and society calls her "difficult" without asking why.

Take Rose, for example. A young woman in her mid-20s, she often faces complications in her relationships. Almost every relationship ends, leading her to think that men lack effort, planning, and future consideration. On the surface, she believes the problem lies with them. But deep down, Rose remembers where her habit of self-criticism began. She questions her appearance, her value, and her life, realizing that these feelings stem from her upbringing.

While growing up, she observed her mother performing countless chores—cooking, cleaning, and running errands—while her father was mostly absent. What Rose absorbed unknowingly was that women were expected to be the main drivers of the household and relationships. In the midst of all this, her mother forgot to care for herself, constantly criticizing her reflection in the mirror.

Rose internalized it. She became critical of herself, too. And what she didn't learn was that relationships need two drivers to thrive, not just one. She unknowingly tried to be that one driver in her relationships—giving more, planning more, doing more—and collapsed every time the effort wasn't reciprocated. Every time in life, she attracted men who were less responsible. She had never seen a normal, healthy relationship. What her parents lived seemed "normal" to her.

Like Rose, many of us are drawn into damaging relationships, only to discover later that unhealthy observations shaped our understanding. The realization often comes much later in life. Similarly, anyone who has struggled with insecurity about their weight, looks, or self-worth should know that these habits often trace back to family and environment, where early jokes, criticism, or neglect shaped how we see ourselves. It all starts there.

For boys, they carry hidden scars too.

. A boy with an overachieving father is constantly compared to others.

. A boy with an irresponsible father matures too quickly, sacrificing dreams to take on responsibilities he never chose.

. A boy with a possessive mother seeks maternal qualities in his partner while constantly struggling with his thoughts.

Sibling dynamics also leave marks. Eldest children may be praised as "golden," while younger ones struggle invisibly. Or the eldest is burdened with responsibility while the younger enjoys freedom. Both carry pain. Often, parents unknowingly create emotional gaps.

That's why I believe anyone who grows up in conflict bears an emotional cost. Trust, repair, and acceptance take time.

The Real Talk

Family is our roots. If we aren't watered, nurtured, and allowed to grow, we feel weakest when we march into the real world. No matter what trauma you carry, the answer always begins with breaking patterns built over the years. Unless you release that heaviness, you won't find peace.

In life, you will meet many people who come from unstable families. But that doesn't give anyone the right to behave badly just because they saw such behavior at home.

And here's the other side: Some people grow up in unhealthy environments yet refuse to be influenced by them. Instead, they turn out to be the most balanced, kind, and content souls you'll ever meet. These people are gems. Never take them for granted.

Detaching yourself from the toxic member of the family is the only way, which no one discusses with you.

Healing Is the Only Way

As we grow, some of us pity ourselves, blaming our parents for failures, imbalance, or rage. But here's the truth: your parents were growing too. Understanding their state of mind, whether happy or unhappy, can provide perspective. Every parent-child relationship has its mix of beneficial and negative aspects. You cannot abandon it completely. Healing, not blame, is the only way forward.

The outcome?

Teens and adults realize gaps in their upbringing—comparison, doubt, insecurity. Every individual deserves care and love to build confidence. Whether privileged or underprivileged doesn't matter. Most anxieties, self-doubt, suppression, and emotional fears originate in childhood.

But society teaches you to hide your scars and carry your wounds, but you must know this. Toxic people, including toxic family members, behave like termites. They slowly eat away your confidence and then blame you for being underconfident. The moment you notice their toxic traits, detach yourself.

Do it immediately. The longer you stay, the deeper they bite. Thankfully, people are talking openly now. But life's complexities won't calm down. They'll increase with technology and advancement. Knowing the source of the problem is the first step. Family is your foundation.

The house you build on it is your choice, your story, your legacy.

Mindset Notes...

1. If something bothers you with a family member, talk and sort it out. The more you keep in your heart, the heavier the pain grows.

2. Practice gratitude, and forgive your parents. Remember, they were young and scared when they had you.

3. Maintain a journal. Write down the most painful moments, and alongside them, write what you learned.

4. If the trauma feels too big to carry alone, talk to a professional. Healing isn't a weakness. It's wisdom.

5. Never marry or commit to someone until you've healed from your wounds. Otherwise, you'll only pass the pain forward. 6. And if you have a healthy family, don't take it for granted. Be grateful, and appreciate it deeply.

Unlike the current chapter, which speaks about family dynamics and their influence on our thoughts and perceptions, self-doubt is different. It is the fear of not being enough, the constant hunger for external validation, and the lack of belief in ourselves.

For many of us, it takes years of exploring and experiencing before we finally learn to accept ourselves, and only then do we begin to truly believe. But here is the truth: not knowing this early in life is also a curse. Deep down, we all know we carry self-doubt—that nagging thought that the other person is better, that we always lack something. The sooner you accept this reality and learn to shrug it off, the freer you become. Otherwise, the boat will sail, and you'll be left standing, still doubting.

It's All in Your Mind—Self-Doubt

"The world will never fully appreciate you. Don't wait for its approval; create your own story and silence the noise around you. If you lack self-confidence, others may also sense that lack in you."

The Hidden Struggle of Adulting

Adulting brings self-doubt and a constant need for approval. We feel incomplete until we receive validation about our appearance, speech, performance, or even the potential success of a startup, love life, friends, and family issues. Occasionally, this craving for approval goes so far that people seek it from pandits, babas, priests, or even occult practices. They trust others more than themselves, doubting their worth repeatedly.

This struggle affects teens, 20-somethings, and adults alike. Some carry low confidence or imposter syndrome for years. Even when we know we've worked diligently, we assume our efforts won't be recognized. Compliments feel fake. We don't see ourselves as worthy of praise.

The Prison of Self-Doubt

The need for approval makes us appear less confident. We rely on others' opinions to shape our identity, feel lacking, and hesitate to take risks. Self-doubt crushes our emotions, desires, and dreams—not because of others, but because of our disbelief.

We dream. We desire. But then we fail. Why? We believe that we won't succeed until everyone else provides their approval. We fear judgment. We imagine them laughing.

That's why so many dreams never take shape. I had a friend who sang beautifully. We encouraged him to take it seriously, maybe even make it his profession. But he convinced himself he was just a bathroom singer. He wanted to, but he never dared. Another friend wanted to start vlogging. His family and peers mocked him, but he remained confident—he simply went for it.

That's the difference. Doubt grows when we let disbelief, shame, and fear outweigh our belief in success. Self-doubt often starts early in life. It comes from inexperience and the fear of failing. People will often tell you, "You're young, be cautious, don't be a fool." However, if there is something in life you genuinely desire—even if it appears minor, such as dyeing your hair red—pursue it.

Every time you overcome doubt, your confidence grows stronger. Those who seem like "big names" now are examples of this. Doubts once surrounded Michelle Obama, Tom Hanks, Dwayne

Johnson, and Amitabh Bachchan. Yet they faced their fears, pushed through uncertainty, and mastered their craft. You can too.

Today, many people shine without the "perfect" body, looks, or skills. Why? Their success is due to their strong belief in themselves. That belief is your power, yet most of us turn it away due to fear of rejection. We fear not being liked. We fear being mocked. It all plays out in our minds.

We become our worst critics and stop appreciating ourselves. Society portrays perfection as the ideal body, skin, and lifestyle. We chase it. But perfection comes with practice. Until you try, you'll never know.

The Cost of Pleasing

Some of us become people pleasers because it feels like the only way to gain confidence. Pleasing others becomes our validation, and until it comes, we feel like we're failing. You might think that unless you constantly help others, you aren't a "good human being." But that's just another form of self-doubt. Helping is beautiful, but not everyone will appreciate it.

Some will overlook your efforts. Some may even use them against you, feeding your self-doubt. Imagine being an intern in a corporate office. You work hard, but your efforts are often dismissed. You start doubting your abilities.

In reality, many know you're talented; sometimes they even feel threatened, so they withhold approval. That's the trap. The more you chase approval, the weaker your confidence becomes. Confidence comes the moment you stop living for others.

People you're trying so diligently to impress today may seem important, but years from now, you'll regret choosing others over yourself. You'll look back and think:

"If only I had trusted my intuition... I would've taken that trip, pursued that passion, said yes to that opportunity, or chosen that person."

My Inner Critic

I spent much of my life doubting my abilities. I believed that even if I produced excellent work, people wouldn't notice. We all have an inner critic, ready to judge, while we silently accept it.

While writing this book, I hear a voice telling me my publisher might reject it and that few will read it. But even after doubts, I still carry hope. That small voice, the one pushing you forward when everything else says stop, keep it. Protect it. Nourish it. That voice is where change begins.

Ask yourself:

. Who are you trying to impress?

. Whose validation are you waiting for?

. Why are you afraid of failure?

We are all on the same journey. Everyone wants to be seen, heard, and understood. Only a few achieve it, not because they lack fears, but because they've learned to tune out the noise. Slowly, doubts dissolve. Childhood Roots

Think back:

. Were you too thin or overweight?

. Too quiet? Did you stammer?

. Did you grow up in a difficult environment?

It all begins there. Your past shows up in your present until you face it. Tackle your fears. Talk about them. Seek help. The past is over; every day is new. Nobody is coming to rescue you. It's your duty to confront the emotions that haunt you.

The Girl Who Wanted to Disappear

I grew up wanting to be unseen. I didn't crave attention, not because I was shy, but because I feared teasing, mocking, and judgment. I struggled with body image. I was skinny, pale, and unhappy with my appearance. It wasn't until people bullied me that I recognized my body image issues were serious.

Even my close family made fun of me, and this criticism became my identity. I would weep as I tried to gain weight and achieve a "perfect" appearance, yet nothing seemed to work. I avoided social gatherings, dressing up, and the spotlight. But in the midst of all the criticism I had faced, fear of rejection became a significant part of me.

Before anyone else could reject me, I rejected myself. Once people sensed my self-doubt, they believed it too. Comments and jokes deepened my self-hatred. I even avoided the gym, fearing people's eyes. Outwardly, I pretended confidence, but inside, I was broken.

The Turning Point

One day, a relative visited my house. My mother asked me to serve tea. After I left, I overheard her say, "She looks like someone with a deadly disease." That comment deeply affected me, bringing me to tears, and that was it. That day I decided to resolve to put an end to it. I had had enough of hiding. I joined the gym, followed a diet, and worked out even when no one was watching.

Slowly, I began showing up for myself. I faced people without fear. I trained rigorously. After months, I gained a healthy weight. Clothes fit better. People noticed and complimented me this time. Had I quit early, I would have missed this transformation. But I didn't. I gained confidence, started modelling, and also professionally became a live show host. I confronted fears and broke through every doubt. I learned it was all in my mind.

What Changed?

I stopped letting self-doubt control me. It was never anyone else's fault; it was mine. I let words take root in my mind. No one really cares. The world notices weakness more than effort. But when you change what bothers you once, the same noise that was against you disappears.

Even today, people comment on my appearance. Few acknowledge my effort. But I don't need validation. I've made peace with my story. It's not just me. Today's generation goes through the same thing—and on a bigger stage. Back then, it was neighbours and relatives. Today, it's trolling, bullying, comments, likes, and social media comparisons.

The pain is the same, only louder. Many young people, when they believe these voices, disown themselves. Writing this chapter takes courage. This isn't fiction; it's my truth. I share it so you don't suffer as I did. Own your voice, flaws, and gifts and rise. It's easy to hate yourself. It takes strength to accept the way you are, walk with confidence, and keep going. I took charge. I worked on everything that made me feel small.

Don't Let Them Win.

People will laugh. They'll criticize. They'll judge your looks, dreams, and failures. It's your responsibility to ignore them. In your teens and 20s, as well as in life generally, everyone offers advice. Everyone tells you about yourself more than you know. Don't listen. Take risks. Fall. Rise. Be answerable to yourself.

Build Your Mindset

Thoughts, choices, and preferences change over time. Don't waste time impressing others.

Instead:

. Work on your strengths.

. Build a mind so strong that no opinion can shake you.

. Clarify your vision to understand your direction.

If you struggle with self-doubt about your body, looks, or personality, accept it, then work on it. Don't ignore it. Face it today.

Practice Self-Love

Self-love shields weaknesses. Allow yourself time. Care for your body, mind, and emotions while respecting others.

Self-doubt might seem harmless, but it's a gateway to envy, negativity, and frustration.

The Final Truth

If you're stuck with body issues, insecurities about finances, relationships, chasing perfection, or low confidence, remember: People will try to suppress you. It's not because you're weak, but rather because confidence can be perceived as a threat to others. Believe in yourself even if others feel uncomfortable.

Don't let them control you. Don't let them win. Educate yourself. Learn skills. Be emotionally sharp. Intelligence and knowledge are unbeatable. Don't seek to please anyone. Be proud of your work. Take small steps. Believe in yourself first; then allow the world to believe in you.

If you have doubts about your appearance, finances, or partner, take steps to address them. Don't overthink—it won't help you grow. Had I learned these lessons earlier, I would have reached my goals sooner. If you aspire to excel in something, please consider taking the first step now.

Mindset Notes...

1. Stand in front of a mirror and accept your flaws.

2. Identify one quality you're proud of.

3. If you wish to change, develop a plan, implement it diligently, and remain committed until completion. Face what scares you most.

4. Turn off social media comments. Don't follow accounts that bother you. Start today.

As we end this chapter and move into the most complicated one that creates unnecessary emotions in humans, self-doubt is a quality that arises from feeling lack, while the next chapter explores the trap of comparison, which generates some of the most difficult emotions, like insecurity, envy, and unworthiness.

Comparison—The Silent Killer

"Everyone has a different timeline in life. Accept it and focus on your path."

We live in a world of invisible races where finish lines are undefined. But the pressure to "reach" is constant. But here is the truth that is often left unspoken: you are on time. You're right on time for your story. Comparison is the thief of joy, yet we all fall into its trap. In life, some people begin their journey at 50, while others seem to achieve everything by their 30s. It can feel suffocating, particularly when you're juggling work, managing responsibilities, and struggling to survive with limited resources.

Society has created a rigid timeline for human progress. Others dictate your life, deciding when you should marry, have kids, or succeed. Somewhere along the way, milestones turned into deadlines. But life isn't a spreadsheet; it's a season, and every season has its own time to bloom. Those who have achieved a place in life will always have opinions about what a "successful" life looks like. The greatest Favor you can do for yourself is to stop listening to them.

Look at your hands. Each finger is a different size. That's not just biology; it's a metaphor. Even your body knows that not everything grows at the same pace. So why should your life? Everyone around you is different, with their own beliefs, cultures, and journeys. Life rarely follows your plan. You are the driver of your journey.

Follow your gut, let your heart guide you, and reach your destination in your time. And if life aligns perfectly with your ideal timeline, consider it a blessing.

The Trap of Social Media Comparison

We live in a world where it takes time to realize your worth. You will make friends along the way, sometimes starting from the same place. One might succeed quickly while the other lags behind.

Social media has become a double-edged sword today, as it displays our lives on a single screen. We scroll through our phones for 5–6 hours a day. Real human connection is disappearing. The new meeting places are messaging apps, and trends are emerging online rather than in the real world. In the middle of all this noise, many people have lost touch with reality. They live in denial, chasing illusions.

If someone buys a new car, others want a better one even if that wasn't their goal. Consumerism is rising, often fueled by influencers. But it's not the influencers' fault; it's the tendency to compare without understanding the full story. We see the highlight reel but ignore the struggles behind it. Success often reflects when someone started, not just where they are now.

I know a friend who buys clothes and bags, sometimes going to thrift shops and buying cheap copy brands just to impress others. However, the amusing part is that the very people she aims to impress are already aware of her sources, and as a result, they mock her without her knowledge.

Why do you want to be part of that circus? Today, the focus has shifted beyond lifestyle; people are also buying followers and creating fake public relations. People are quietly attempting to demonstrate their soft power, as if having more followers is a sign of respect. But ask yourself, is it? Really necessary? Even individuals who don't engage in digital activities can succumb to comparison traps.

A 9-to-5 employee may question their job after seeing an influencer making more money, forgetting the pressure, anxiety, trolling, and lack of job security behind the feed. Nothing you see online is as effortless as it looks. If you have passion and discipline, pursue it. But never fall into the trap of constant comparison. The world doesn't need another copy of someone else's life. It needs you and your story.

Stop Comparing—The Highlight Reel Isn't the Whole Story Esha's Story

Esha excelled both in academics and extracurriculars. Her mother constantly pushed her to seek bigger platforms. At 15, she participated in a reality dance show, which led to numerous opportunities. Offers poured in, and she left her education midway to chase her dreams. Now,

Esha shares her wins on social media. People compare their lives to hers, thinking, "We're the same age; why am I not there yet?" But they don't see her longing. She envies friends who went to college, built friendships, and lived carefree student lives. Her success came with sacrifices. Early success without proper education or emotional guidance can make someone arrogant, emotionally unstable, isolated, and constantly drained. Work pressures often lead to harmful coping mechanisms, including substance abuse.

Despite having enormous wealth and fame, they yearn for a simpler life and to spend quality time with their loved ones. People see them as sensations, not human beings, and occasionally, they involve themselves with toxic people for emotional support.

This explains why the prospect of a better life always seems more appealing. Everyone experiences some form of lack. No one has everything. That's why it's wise to focus on what's in your hands now, instead of being swept away by the illusion that someone else is happier or luckier.

Alex's Story

Alex, a guy in his 20s, worked night shifts. Tired of the same workplace for years, frustrated with the timings, and coming from a modest background, he scrolled through social media every night. Friends were partying, travelling, buying cars, and getting married. Alex felt depressed and had FOMO, thinking he couldn't enjoy life despite working tirelessly.

To make his life look more intriguing to his friends, he started taking out loans to buy branded clothes, took breaks to go on vacations, and posted pictures all showing he was keeping up with everyone. Months later, he was anxious and depressed and buried in debt; he realized he was imitating someone else's life. While his previous life may have appeared monotonous, it provided him with a sense of peace.

Meanwhile, his social media accounts praised his "great life," but in reality, he was struggling to pay off loans and facing pressure from banks. He lost his peace, freedom, and integrity when he tried to fit in.

Many young people in developing countries compare their lives to those in wealthier nations, believing life is "easier" there. But the truth is, inflation rises everywhere, stress touches everyone, and balance always takes effort.

Living abroad doesn't erase the longing for home, family, and culture. Social media may display captivating 60-second snippets, but these are merely highlights and do not represent a complete life. Life isn't "easy" anywhere.

The key is to set your own priorities and stop worrying about what the world is doing.

The Psychology of Comparison

Comparison is not new. Thousands of years ago, humans competed only for survival; those who had the better weapon, more food, or a higher status in the tribe. Back then, it was basic. But today? We compare vacations, brands, lifestyles, and home aesthetics. It has become a battlefield of appearances.

Those who are content with a simple life are judged and called out in different ways. But the truth is, you don't have to be overly decorated with low intelligence. It was always about having a simple life and high thinking.

This perspective reflects the old-money view, which values wealthy wisdom over mere appearances. Look at the Middle East today. The lifestyle industry is skyrocketing there. But have you seen the other cities of those countries? The reality is different. They only market what appeals to you and entices you to spend, sometimes leading to excessive credit use.

The issue of comparison is now widespread. Whether it's fake followers, fake luxury, or online "power couples" who appear flawless on screen but remain unfaithful in real life, the issue of comparison is everywhere. Consider whether you truly need to be a part of this spectacle. Comparison today is a trap dressed as aspiration.

Stop Comparing.

If you see friends travelling or enjoying life while you're working a 9-to-5 job or struggling, know this: constant comparison leads to depression. People compare wealth, lifestyle, and success—in person or online. This generation, in particular, engages in endless comparisons regarding travel, relationships, cars, clothes, and more.

Girls compare beauty and partners; guys compare status and wealth. Most do not celebrate what they have. Everyone is living a double life, one reel and one real. This constant need to compare and showcase is toxic to the mind. You don't know someone's inner struggles. Even those who appear happy might be fighting battles. Therefore, stop comparing your achievements, looks, lifestyle, or path to someone else's. It's not always what it seems. What you see online is the trailer, not the full movie.

Some people seem to succeed easily, but even that is often the result of years of sacrifice. Everyone has a story of pain, struggle, and growth. Everyone earns their success in their time. You'll arrive there too when you work for yourself. Life is not a race. You'll hear noise, doubt yourself, and fear falling behind. But the journey is about becoming you, not being first. Everyone is precisely where they're meant to be.

Expectation hurts.

If envy or anxiety grows, take a break. Accept your life. Stop blaming. Focus on solutions to change what you can. After a point, no one rescues you; it's you vs. you. Choose your niche. Become your own leader. Put your heart into everything. People who embrace struggle often define their own terms in life. Pause, look around, and appreciate how far you've come, even if it's not where you expected.

And here's the thing about comparison: it doesn't just bug you in your 20s. It also makes a difference in your 30s and 40s. In your 30s, comparison shifts to promotions, marriage, kids, or buying a home.

Later, it may be about financial security, health, or even your children's achievements. Society and social media continue to feed this cycle at every stage. People still feel anxious and experience FOMO when they see others living the life they once wanted or the life they can't have. Society will keep creating timelines. Early success doesn't always mean lasting fulfilment. Some bloom later and shine brighter. Social media shows highlights, not behind-the-scenes battles.

Never compare your reality with someone else's edited life. You're not here to rush. You're here to rise. You evolve and succeed when you rise at your pace, guided by your purpose. You are in control.

You will encounter obstacles and criticism, yet only you possess the ability to reach your desired destination. Make your journey special. Embrace every detour and lesson. That's what makes you a rare gem—not just another diamond.

Mindset Notes...

1. Practice gratitude— List three things you are genuinely pleased and thankful for. This creates peace and happiness within.

2. Reduce your social media consumption—what appears online is merely a preview, not the complete story. Stop confusing highlights with reality.

3. Observe yourself—Notice what you mostly compare in life: money, looks, lifestyle, or relationships. This helps you focus on your true priorities. flow.

Part II

Habits & Discipline...

HABIT—THE Seeds to Your Future

"Habits are your invisible army. They fight for you when motivation dies. You don't rise to the level of your dreams you fall to the level of your habits."

If I could go back in time and offer my 20-year-old self a piece of advice, it would be this: cultivate better habits now, rather than waiting for later. The earlier we understand that small habits make life more rewarding and less stressful, the better.

When we first enter adulthood, no one informs us that we could solve half of our struggles by vigilantly monitoring and consistently building our habits. Don't wait for a specific or a difficult moment to transform your life. The habits you're creating today, whether consciously or carelessly, are shaping the person you'll wake up as five years from now.

Your 20s often feel like a time of recklessness and self-centeredness. You believe in your knowledge. Advice sounds like background noise. You brush it off, thinking you've got plenty of time. I comprehend it—I was that person too.

I remember waking up one morning in my 20s, feeling drained without accomplishing any major task. My to-do list seemed to mock me. My energy felt drained, yet I hadn't done any real work. That was the day I realized habits don't drain energy; the lack of them does. But one day, you'll look back and realize how foolish it was to miss opportunities disguised as "boring routines."

Small Habits, Big Impact

Making your bed, exercising, or adhering to a clean diet may seem like small, almost silly tasks. But here's the truth: these are the foundations of your life. Effective habits aren't just tools; they're armour. Every individual you admire who has achieved success in life did not merely possess dreams; they also established a framework.

From athletes who relentlessly train to monks who rise at dawn to meditate to entrepreneurs who attribute their success to their routines, habits transcend borders, cultures, and careers. They're universal weapons for growth.

Why Most People Fail at Building Habits

The reason most people fail at building habits is due to a lack of validation. No one claps when you wake up at 6 a.m. People don't congratulate you for abstaining from junk food or for declining invitations to late-night parties. That silence is why people quit. They're chasing praise—not purpose.

Habit-building is a solo game. No audience means no likes. You vow to change tomorrow, but when alone, you ignore the alarm. You scroll. You delay. Look at the people entering their 30s and 40s with quiet confidence. They didn't stumble upon luck. They committed to themselves when no one else was watching. That's the hardest part—showing up for yourself without applause.

The Story of the Athlete Who Failed

Robin, in his 20s, loved football. Watching matches was his passion, and he dreamed of being on the field himself. But his habits never matched his dream. To be a professional, passion is not enough—you need focus, strict discipline, and self-control. This entails maintaining regular sleep patterns, maintaining a healthy diet, and engaging in consistent training. You cannot consistently stay up late gaming, binge-watching, or partying every weekend and then expect to perform at a professional level.

Robin never built the habits required. He had the desire but not the discipline. And that's why his dream stayed a dream. Life isn't made up of enormous moments. It's built from thousands of tiny ones. And in those tiny moments, your routine either saves you or breaks you.

Why Routine Matters Remember

When we were kids? Moms set our eating schedules. Schools gave us timetables. Our lives were guided. But the moment we step into adulthood, we're on our own. And most people? They never learn how to set their structure. They start the year with goals. By day three, they've already broken them. Why? Distractions take control. Back then, focus was natural.

Today, the focus is on a fight. And here's the challenging truth: milestones can only be achieved if you stay consistent in your routine. Even if you win an award today, tomorrow you still have to wake up and follow the same structure. That's why you should choose a hobby, learn new skills, and make them part of your daily life.

It keeps every day intriguing and provides you with something to look forward to. Studies indicate that habits automate up to 40% of our daily actions. That means nearly half your life runs on autopilot, so imagine if your autopilot was designed to help you win

The 21-Day Habit Challenge

Science says it takes 21 days to build a habit. I tested this myself, and it works. For most of my life, I never had a proper morning routine. My days would start messy and end the same way. I took the 21-day challenge.

As someone who is not naturally inclined to mornings, I compelled myself to set an alarm, wake up at the same time each day, have breakfast before noon, and repeat this routine consistently until it became a habit. I kept myself accountable by tracking my progress and ticking off each day. Now, these practices feel natural to me.

I regret not starting sooner—I discovered these techniques much later in life. Don't wait. Your 20s are the best time to test and lock in habits. The earlier you start, the lighter and easier life feels later.

Aaron vs. Roman: A Tale of Two Twenties

Aaron and **Roman** were the same age, but their 20s couldn't have been more different. Aaron woke up late, skipped meals, scrolled endlessly, delayed tasks, avoided exercise, smoked, and partied almost every night. His life was messy, unplanned, and stressful. Screens dominated his days, leaving him frustrated and scattered. Roman lived differently.

Weekdays were structured with early mornings, gym sessions, preplanned meals, and focused work. Weekends, he reserved for fun. He handled chores, planned, and avoided unnecessary chaos. By the time they hit 30, Roman was ready to start his venture. Aaron was still struggling, feeling irritable and frustrated as he tried to discover the foundation he had never built. The difference wasn't luck, talent, or opportunity. It was a habit.

During the first half of my 20s, I felt a lot like Aaron—messy, distracted, and still figuring things out. This feeling is completely normal. However, once I discovered my niche, I began to understand the true importance of establishing positive habits and effectively managing time. Roman's life may look robotic, but you don't have to imitate somebody else's routine. The secret is balance: enjoy your 20s, but stay in control.

Sleep: The Most Ignored Habit

If you've been feeling fatigued, cranky, unmotivated, or gaining weight, it could be from lack of sleep. One week without proper rest can destroy your mind and body. Severe sleep deprivation can literally kill you. In today's digital world, sleep is the most neglected habit. Earlier generations never compromised on it.

But we gamble our sleep for entertainment, endless scrolling, or late-night hustle culture. Sleep resets your brain and heals your body. A baby's sleep is protected because it's essential for growth. As adults, it's no different. Fatigue. Memory loss. Early aging. Anxiety. Poor sleep is the root cause of all these issues. Want to change your life? Try sleeping on time for just seven days. The difference will shock you.

Positive Habits = Non-Negotiable Tools

They fuel your mind. Strengthen your body. Stabilize your emotions. Negative habits often come from stress and laziness. Instead of choosing what heals us (walking, meditating, journaling, talking), we choose what numbs us (smoking, drinking, scrolling). Most people complain about their situation but refuse to do what fixes it. Flip the pattern. Focus on small wins. Develop one positive habit. Take each day as it comes.

The Outcome

What is the most significant insight gained from developing strong habits? They make you self-reliant, organized, and reliable. These small, daily habits not only transform your routine but also help shape your true self. You evolve into someone others admire, embodying a strong and influential mindset.

Final Truth

Let's be real. If you are reading this, your next action will likely be to scroll or relax. That's how powerful habits are; they decide your future without you even realizing it. Before you scroll, pause. Write down one habit you'll commit to today.

That small pause could change your entire future. Take your time. Pick habits gradually. It's not too late unless you keep acting like it is. Build your routine. Stick with it. Ten years from now, even if you're not rich or famous, at least you won't be unhealthy, anxious, or burnt out. That kind of peace in your later years is priceless. Routine won't guarantee you a palace, but it will provide you with a clear head, a calm mind, and control over your life. And honestly, that's already winning.

Mindset Notes...

Write down three habits you currently indulge in. Be brutally honest with yourself.

Create a note (digital or physical) where you list:

1. Identify the habits that are causing you harm.

2. List the habits you want to develop. Pick one habit and commit to the 21-Day Habit Challenge. Announce it to a friend, on social media, or even in your journal.

That accountability makes you consistent.

1. Note down the habit you are proud of.

2. Identify the new habit you wish to adopt.

Keep a notebook or tracker to tick off every day you show up. Even if you skip, don't quit. Just come back from where you left.

The greatest challenge isn't just forming a habit; it's killing the ones that delay your progress. The most troublesome are procrastination and laziness, which can silently dominate your 20s if you allow them to. And that's precisely what we'll explore in the next chapter.

Laziness and Procrastination: The Quiet Killers of Progress

"Laziness is a man's greatest enemy, and procrastination is what most people call 'bad luck.' But the truth is simple: your life didn't fall behind because of fate. It happened because you didn't show up when opportunities knocked on your door."

Have you ever cancelled plans or missed a meeting just because you felt lazy? Have you delayed workouts even after paying for the gym? Have you ever committed yourself to begin a new routine on Monday, only to repeatedly postpone it until the entire year has passed?

And then, one day, you browse social media and observe your friends' receiving awards or creating the life you envisioned, accompanied by a sense of regret for the time you have squandered. That's what laziness and procrastination do. They quietly kill progress. Have you ever wasted an entire day in bed? Have you ever found yourself rushing through assignments just minutes before the deadline?

If the answer is yes, you're not alone. These habits creep in disguised as rest or distraction. Slowly, they stop being one-time excuses and start becoming your lifestyle. And your lifestyle shapes your future. Simply showing up on time and with consistency can win most battles in life.

In your teens and twenties, especially during a time filled with distractions, achieving a goal and consistently sticking to it has become one of the hardest challenges. People want instant gratification and instant reward. Some start but quit midway because they lack patience, self-belief, or the willingness to wait. In both cases, progress is lost, confidence fades, and self-worth takes a hit.

5-Minute Conquer

The fact is, laziness and procrastination are long-term losses. Initially, you don't even realize these habits are killing your motivation. It's a hit you only notice later in life. When you look back, all you'll see are gloomy memories, a guilt trap, and regret for not being active.

And what if those five minutes you surrendered to delay could have been avoided? That harmless delay of just five minutes can steal your entire life goals. The mindset of "I can do it tomorrow" changes the moment you wake up from these chains. There's a saying: tomorrow never comes. And those who keep delaying things for tomorrow know it all too well.

Your twenties are the vibrant, tumultuous years of life, characterized by a desire to socialize, relax, and postpone responsibilities indefinitely. You delay trips, duties, health, even checkups, and somehow, it feels acceptable. But life is unpredictable. For once, adopt the attitude of doing everything today. Make it a habit. You'll notice something powerful: simply fulfilling your duties right away gives you energy, focus, and control. You feel charged. You feel unstoppable.

Ryan's Story

Ryan was a talented travel agent. His life looked perfect with travel, creativity, and money. But he had one flaw. He never saved or invested. He spent recklessly on gadgets, perfumes, and clothes. His parents kept telling him to invest, purchase insurance, and save something. He always delayed. "Later. I'll always have work. Let me live my life first," he'd say. But life doesn't provide warnings.

Something unpredictable happened. COVID-19, the lockdown, and the world paused. Initially, like everyone, Ryan thought it would be lifted in a few days. But days turned into months. Projects were cancelled. Overnight, he was jobless. His bank balance shrank day by day. Surrounded by his gadgets and shoes, he pondered, "What is the purpose of all this? If only I had saved some money." With no backup, Ryan became a delivery agent. Harsh, exhausting work taught him humility, discipline, and the value of every single penny.

When work finally returned, he wasn't the same person. He stopped delaying. He started saving. He started investing. Now Ryan plans for tomorrow while enjoying his present. He discovered that life is unpredictable, presenting unexpected challenges at any given time. That lesson hit deeper than any failure ever could.

Laziness Has No Age: Martin's Story

Martin was well-settled and had created enormous wealth in his life. Now in his late forties, he possesses money, land, and comfort. But his body is failing. He has arthritis. His bone density is low. All his life, he focused on building his bank account, but he skipped his health.

He postponed going to the gym, lacked a consistent exercise routine, ate poorly, and smoked to relieve stress. People believe that possessing wealth enables one to recover health, but their assumption is not accurate. You can settle hospital bills, certainly; however, your condition will persist indefinitely. Having a balanced life is key. Although Martin worked diligently for his passion, he could have achieved a better balance by prioritizing his health.

Later in life, he understood the real wealth is health, something he had taken for granted. Now Martin is gradually doing light exercise but often regrets it. He says if he hadn't been inactive, if he had worked out regularly or joined some recreational activity, he could've at least enjoyed the wealth he worked so diligently for. This is the future anyone can have if they delay forming proper habits.

My Honest Confession

In my twenties, I too struggled with routine. I lost opportunities due to my tendency to snooze alarms and wake up late. But when I realized my laziness wasted not only my time but also other people's, I had to change.

One of the greatest lies we tell ourselves when we are young is "I have time. I'll do it later." I believed that too, until life hit. During COVID-19, when everything paused, I realized the truth. If I had built stronger habits earlier, financially, emotionally, and physically, I would have saved myself years of chaos.

It's Deeper Than Just Being Lazy

Laziness today isn't what it used to be. Growing up as millennials, life was simpler. Friendships were offline. Distractions were fewer. But today, we're living in the most distracted era ever. While we perceive our days to be shorter and time to be passing quickly, the reality is that gadgets and social media steal our valuable hours. They leave us drained and exhausted.

We often choose to skip meeting people in person. Meals are left to sit on the table for too long, and we frequently take our phones into the restroom, oblivious to how much time we waste scrolling through shorts and reels.

As a result, we find ourselves in a panic about being late, which leads to delays in eating, sleeping, and working out. We allow swipes and scroll to control our lives. Spending a single moment on TikTok, YouTube, or Netflix can quickly consume our entire day. Time, peace, confidence, and focus slip away while you sit and watch others live their lives.

Social media is not a threat. How we use it is. Some people use it to build careers, while many use it to escape life.

Mindset Notes...

1. Start your day right. Establish a wake-up time and stick to it. Take a bath early. It wakes your body and mind.

2. Do the difficult thing first. Write down the task you've been avoiding and finish it before anything else.

3. Plan your day. Create a routine with time slots. Follow it for a week, then tweak it to keep it fresh.

4. Control your environment. Don't sink into the couch or stay glued to gadgets. Keep a water tumbler beside you. Small movements keep you awake.

5. Use reminders wisely. Set alarms for both small and big tasks to stay on track.

6. Protect your focus. Avoid using your phone in the bathroom or while eating. You'll save hours every week just because of this.

Final Wake-Up Call

A delay today will turn into regret tomorrow. Understand the power of now. Laziness and procrastination don't just steal your time. They quietly push you into your comfort zone.

At first, it feels safe, easy, and risk-free. But stay there too long, and growth stops. Your most important years of life are not meant for remaining a seed. It's time to establish roots, break through the soil, and reach for the sunlight.

Please make the most of these years without delay. Do it now. In the next chapter, we'll see how the comfort zone, which looks harmless, can quietly become the most significant hurdle to facing your fears and truly growing.

Comfort Now, Regret Later

"If you want a life beyond ordinary you must step out of the comfortable mindset that keeps you ordinary."

There comes a point in life when you feel trapped in habits and duties. Your heart wants more, but courage doesn't show up. Fear whispers that it's safer to stay where you are, leading you to live the same day, in the same loop, without achieving anything new. You feel the discomfort of risk, and doubt in your success grows. If this has happened to you, recognize it. You've surrendered to a life of mediocrity. You're at a crossroads: leap, or be stuck in mediocrity.

What Is the Comfort Zone?

The comfort zone is a complex trap. For someone who wants to grow emotionally, mentally, and consciously, stress over change can make expansion feel impossible. Take this example. A person wants to learn how to drive but fears crashing. To avoid the stress, they never even try. They stay stuck in the same spot, wishing for change but never moving toward it. Now flip it. A person wants to go hiking but is afraid of heights.

Fear tells them to quit, yet they push through anyway. That moment signifies more than just hiking; it signifies breaking free from the confines of comfort. One person lets fear lock them in. The other uses fear as a signal to grow. Most people choose comfort to avoid stress or anxiety, but staying trapped in your mental loop is the most dangerous decision you can make.

Why We Stay Stuck

Fear of change is the main reason. Your comfort zone is like a cocoon. To grow, you have to shed old habits, relationships, and environments that no longer serve you. Just like a caterpillar turning into a butterfly, you must embrace change repeatedly. I've seen so many people dream of big things: success, freedom, a better life. Yet they stay trapped in small, convenient bubbles. They talk, but they never dare. Why? They've convinced themselves that this is the nature of life. Their mind feels safe without pressure.

Deep down, they fear they're not strong enough to handle new stress: to learn a skill, switch careers, or move to a new place. The modern world doesn't help. Everything is delivered to your doorstep. You can scroll endlessly, binge-watch for hours, and obtain dopamine boosts from notifications, yet feel as though you are accomplishing something when in fact you are doing nothing. It feeds laziness. It feeds procrastination. And it all starts with comfort.

Stories of Comfort and Risk Anum and the Relationship That Got Too Comfortable

Anum had been in a long-term relationship with Matt. Despite every heated and abusive argument, they had, she continued to hold onto hope. She was deeply aware that Matt had changed since their first meeting years ago. She believed she could replace the missing part and that his behaviour toward her was normal, as he looked stressed.

But the real problem was one-sided attachment and the comfort she clung to, while the other had already emotionally evolved and moved on. She waited for him to change. She adjusted. She convinced herself it was okay if he avoided her, as long as they were still together.

Matt knew this. He knew Anum wouldn't leave. And that's where the damage began. When you're young, attachment can grow so strong that even when love fades, the fear of starting over feels heavier than the weight of a dead relationship. You normalize the pain.

Suddenly, it feels easier to drag a dying relationship than to rebuild your life. That's what comfort does. It makes you choose familiar suffering over unknown freedom. In relationships where you endure, chances are you lose yourself. The day you take the first step to walk away from what drains you is the day you meet a fresh version of yourself.

Akay and the Safe Job

Humans are not trees. We aren't meant to stay rooted forever. **Akay** worked in Mumbai at an IT firm. In his mid-twenties, after completing post-graduation, he landed a decent job. On paper, it had everything: a satisfactory salary, stable work, and weekends free to chill. Life was pleasant.

But after a year, every day looked the same. Wake up. Same bus. Same office. Swipe the card. Same desk. Same work. Every morning when he took that bus, the potholes he saw and the billboards he passed were the same repeating cycle, like a never-ending loop.

He wanted a shift in life, and all he needed was that first step to change it. He stayed. Bills were paid on time, weekends were comfortable, but inside, he knew it wasn't enough. He was young, passionate, and energetic. Now was the time to take risks, explore, and put himself out there. But fear always sounded louder than his dreams.

This isn't just Akay. Thousands of people in their twenties, and even some later in life, retreat into comfort zones without even realizing it. Spare time is spent scrolling, gaming, and streaming, numbing ourselves instead of exploring. Only a few break that pattern, test their skills, and chase what truly pulls at them.

Breaking the Pattern

Comfort itself isn't wrong. Suppressing your desires, motivation, and passion is wrong. Almost all of us have, at some point, chosen comfort over desire. The stories above show common situations. In relationships, too much comfort can make you blind to abuse or neglect. Some people spend years in draining relationships instead of building themselves. That's why the moment you sense something wrong; you must make a gradual shift.

Don't wait for things to change drastically. If something is truly right, it will grow without you begging for it. Similarly, seeking growth but expecting no challenges is a fantasy. Many remain stuck with the same pay check, the same people, and a monotonous life. Breaking the comfort zone means breaking the pattern.

Yes, there are harmless comfort zones: staying home instead of partying, eating familiar food, and keeping a small circle of positive friends. They keep you grounded and modest. But if you desire growth—financial, physical, mental, or spiritual—you must break the comfort zone. Break the Loop.

Your comfort zone:

. Kills motivation

. Makes you mediocre

. Suppresses your dreams

Convinces you to settle for whatever you have Only a handful manage to break free. Why? This problem is because only a select few are prepared to confront their fears and take calculated risks.

. Face fear.

. Risk failure.

Live uncomfortably for something greater. The rest stay behind with excuses, regrets, and "maybe next month." Some don't move because they care too much about what others will say. Remember, you either live with the discomfort of discipline today or the lifelong regret of not showing up for yourself.

We're human. Change doesn't happen overnight. Awareness is the first step. Start small. Keep promises to yourself. Don't delay the little things. The habit of showing up every single day will serve you for a lifetime.

Mindset Notes...

1. Face the change you fear. Write down one change you constantly desire but avoid because fear blocks you.

2. Act boldly. Implement one small but uncomfortable action this week, even if it causes discomfort.

3. Renew yourself. Change your attire, style, or routine. Sometimes, upgrading your external appearance can inspire changes within you.

Comfort is a chain that will tie you forever, while courage is a breakthrough that will introduce you to your new version.

Part III
Relationships & Identity...

Bodies Touched, Souls Ignored

"In today's time, people are more ready to commit their body than their soul. And that's exactly where heartbreaks, distractions, and depressions begin.

We're in such a rush to explore someone's body that we forget to take responsibility for their feelings. Love didn't change; we're the ones who made it instant."

Why are we starving for love when it's right here between us? Why do we crave peace but keep chasing chaos? Why do we wait to update our relationship status online instead of being truly present with each other in real life? We aspire to present ourselves as a "power couple," yet internally, we feel powerless in matters of love. We care more about showing others we're in love than actually being in love.

Modern love is not dead; it's just confused. And the truth is, love was never complicated. We made it that way. Many people believe the myth that your twenties are only for fun and marriage comes later. But let me break that. A friend of mine and her boyfriend have been together since their teens. Both came from humble backgrounds, simple vibes, and less fuss. They got married at 23. People questioned them and mocked their choice, but they stayed unaffected.

Today, they've started their own matchmaking firm. They say when you discover the right partner early in life, your focus actually increases. For them, marriage wasn't a trap; it was an anchor. In the era of dating apps, they proved marriage still holds value. So don't blindly follow rules made by others. Create your own.

The Reality of Modern Freedom

The reality is, according to global studies, fewer people are opting for marriage. They prefer to stay single, glorify hookups, and call it freedom. Yet this same freedom is pushing suicide rates, crimes, and even murders. Everything is interconnected. Humans are social animals. We thrive only through emotions, intimacy, and love. If you bare your body to almost everyone, you end up hollow inside, like cardboard. And then you cry that nobody loves you.

Truth is, you chose it yourself. Not aiming for marriage is your personal choice, but having one stable partner and being deeply devoted to one person is what keeps your mind healthy. Meet five people at a time and see how exhausted you feel. Meet one person and notice the glow it leaves on your face. At least be present with one instead of welcoming chaos, distractions, and health issues like STDs, infections, and HIV. Remember: what provides you pleasure can also cause you pain.

The Illusion of Modern Love

Love is deeply personal. Its meaning changes as we grow. It's acceptable to feel something for someone once and then feel differently with time. As you evolve, your priorities, your energy, and your understanding of love change too. But let's face it. This generation isn't numb. You feel deeply. But you often confuse attention with affection, lust with love, and companionship with commitment. Hookups, rapid replies, late-night texts, and reels often obscure real connection.

Swipes, Sex, and Shortcuts

We're living in a world where people are being selected and rejected like shopping bags. A quick swipe left, a heart emoji, and suddenly, you're "talking." But is it love? Let's be real. What many call love today is often just a combination of desire, distraction, and a craving for validation.

Physical attraction is not love. Late-night conversations are not intimacy. Sex is not connected. Understand this: there is a deep connection between your physical body, your mental space, and your emotional well-being. When you casually involve yourself with someone without even knowing their trauma, their story, or their truth, you don't just walk away the next day like nothing happened.

You walk away, becoming more distracted. You leave feeling somewhat more detached. Too many people think hooking up is harmless, just part of exploring life. But they forget that every time you become physically close, you're also exchanging energy.

You're inviting distraction, emotional confusion, and sometimes dependence. That's a risky game to play in a world already grappling with focus. Some people say, "Everyone's doing it." But that doesn't mean it's right for you. You are not everyone. You are not a swipe. You are someone's peace. You serve as a secure haven for someone.

Digital Love, Real Consequences

This generation is getting emotionally attached to people they've never met and have just exchanged texts, memes, and filtered selfies with. People are building. bonds through DMs and deciding their future based on typing speed and Instagram aesthetics. There's even a term now: virtual love. It seems intriguing, doesn't it? However, it can become dangerous if not handled properly.

Let me tell you about Lisa. She was an interior designer from London who met a guy named Rock on a dating app. Rock was charming, rich-looking, and said all the right things. They chatted and exchanged photos, music, and daily updates. Slowly, Lisa started imagining a life with him.

Then came the twist. He said he had a medical emergency and needed money. Lisa sent him £10,000. And then he vanished. Heartbroken and confused, Lisa spent weeks trying to track him down, only to realize she had fallen victim to a sophisticated scam.

Determined to reclaim her sense of self, she began sharing her story online to warn others about the dangers of online dating and the importance of being cautious with personal information. Stories like Lisa's are everywhere. Fake promises are trapping real people. And let's not ignore the darker side. Dating apps have also led to instances of assault, blackmail, and even murder.

These apps are designed to keep you hooked. But what about the creators of these apps? They're probably spending time with their families while you chase illusions. I'm not against digital love. People do discover true love on social networking sites, like my sister, who is happily married now. She found her love through these platforms. But she wasn't seeking it. It was destined. I recall how apprehensive and cautious she was before meeting the individual who ultimately proved to be authentic.

Finding love on a digital platform is debatable, but what people often lack is the patience to truly get to know someone and understand their real personality beyond their profile. My sister was wise. She did her homework. She didn't believe everything she saw; she believed in what she felt. She researched him. She was practical.

And that's how she chose her Mr. Right. We've made significant progress from matrimonial sites, where marriage was the primary goal, to dating apps, where the primary goal is often attention or validation. It's no surprise that love feels confusing. You're not broken for feeling that way.

Stories That Speak

Now meet **Nina**. She came from a tough background but wanted to change her reality. She believed that marrying a wealthy man was the quickest way to change her circumstances. So, she groomed herself, faked an elite lifestyle on social media, and joined dating platforms to attract wealthy men.

One day, she found her match. She pretended to be innocent, helpless, and in love. The man, genuine and trusting, married her. But after some time, Nina was bored. She had everything she once prayed for: money and security. But she still felt empty. Love that is based on pretense does not endure. Now, she's stuck with a life she chose for survival, not for love.

Then there's **Orry**. Orry, a flamboyant guy, constantly swipes left and right on dating apps. His routine consisted of casual dates and casual hookups. His friends would warn him, "This lifestyle isn't beneficial for your mental health." But Orry would laugh it off, saying he was just passing time and focused on building his startup.

Then one day, he met a girl. She was different. Intriguing. She didn't respond to his flirty texts. She wasn't interested in casual attention; she was bold and ambitious. And that got to him.

Orry was stuck, not in her, but in what she represented. She didn't chase, and that challenged his whole identity. He tried everything: gestures, efforts, and persistence. But she never gave him the same energy. He got emotionally involved, maybe for the first time genuinely. And it broke him. He lost focus. He got distracted. It took him nearly three years to get back on his feet.

The Reality of Emotional Timing

Here's the reality. You may believe you can dictate the timing and manner in which love manifests in your life. But emotional connections, love, and friendship often creep in silently. You don't realize it until you've given too much. And when it doesn't work out, you're the one left questioning everything. And remember this. You can buy clothes, gadgets, accessories, and even makeup online.

However, when it comes to love, nothing surpasses the sensation of having the person you are attracted to sitting right in front of you. Nothing compares to the conversation that flows between two people over coffee. Love was, is, and will always remain a traditional entity.

Love, But No Responsibility

This generation is addicted to instant gratification: instant food, instant money, and instant love. But love is not instant. It's a commitment. A process. A responsibility. Everyone desires the positive aspects of love; however, when it comes to consistently showing up each day, individuals often withdraw. That's why distractions like DMs, comparisons, and scrolling have replaced real presence. That's why so many breakups, divorces, and broken hearts exist.

Feeding Loneliness with Fantasy

The loneliness we see today and the depression people post about mostly shy away. from naming the real truth: people are using them like commodities. I remember a friend of mine, married but living long distance. He hid his marital status, flirted, texted, and pretended to be a bachelor. He told me how these dating apps were helping him "survive" loneliness.

But let me tell you: that wasn't survival. It became his lifestyle. Even if he and his wife stayed together, he'd still cheat. Cheating no longer stemmed from loneliness; it had become a habit. The present day is the age of complexities.

Some people hide their relationships, others over-display them, and both end up complicating things. You may socialize with many individuals, but it is important to discern who is truly worth investing in for a lifelong relationship and who is merely suitable for casual companionship in the short term.

From the Heart of a Millennial

The importance of understanding this early in life stems from the fact that I am a millennial. We were not born into a world with social media. We didn't grow up in the digital era. We were raised in simpler times. If you ever engage in conversation with a millennial or simply observe the music and films from our era, the '90s to early 2010s, you will recognize the extent of our profound romanticism.

We romanticized everything: the rain, handwritten letters, and heartbreaks. We believed in falling truly and deeply, often without realizing how practical or brutal the world could be. Yes, many of us went through heartbreaks that shaped us. But today, everyone lives dual lives, one in reality and one on social media.

Your profile has become your business card. Individuals assess your value based on your postings: your appearance, your acquaintances, your leisure activities, and your overall demeanor. But remember: connection and energy are only felt in real moments.

In conversations. In closeness. Love was never meant to be instant. Love is a gradual process, not a quick fix. I wish I had known earlier how important it is to read people before forming emotional attachments. We often become stuck in toxic relationships not because we love the person, but because we're deeply attached.

Protecting Your Peace

My esteemed ones, you will be gentle, receptive, enthusiastic, and filled with love, and that is truly wonderful. However, avoid succumbing to the influence of others. Especially avoid falling into lust that is disguised as love. Recognize the warning signs.

Hold your grip. Protect your peace. Love is not a chase; it's a slow unfolding. Not all screen time is connected. Occasionally, you're just feeding loneliness with fantasy.

You think it's love, but it's just someone filling a gap for now. Too much exposure to soft porn, fake dating standards, or emotional baiting drains your clarity and peace. It might not feel harmful, but slowly, it steals your focus, your energy, and your sense of self.

Love is not supposed to leave you confused, anxious, or insecure. It should bring peace, grounding, and inner joy.

The world may glorify fast love, but slow love is still real. Slow love grows, breathes, forgives, and builds. If you are still awaiting that form of love, then you are in a favorable position. Good. The delay is a sign that you are in search of something exceptional.

Stay rare.

. Choose depth over drama.

. Choose truth over trends.

. Choose peace over chaos.

The right kind of love will hold not only your hand but also your soul.

The Human Need for Connection

As we learn in this chapter, the world is shifting its mindset toward instant gratification, chasing quick highs, making less effort in real connection, and drowning deeper in anxiety and depression. Relationships today are often defined by chats, swipes, DMs, likes, and comments. But no matter how easy these things look, one truth never changes: the human craving for real connection.

In this fast-paced world, generations may long to build strong social bonds, yet many live in denial. In the next chapter, we'll talk about connection, not the digital illusion, but the real bonds of family and marriage, and how ignoring them is taking a toll on human psychology.

Marriage in the Modern World

"People have completely confused a wedding with a marriage. A wedding is just a one-day event, but a marriage is a lifelong commitment that survives only on understanding, patience, and loyalty."

The extension of human life is formed through love. You are born out of love; when a man and a woman come together, a child grows. The world itself thrives through love, connection, and the unseen energy between us. As we grow older, we all imagine the perfect partner. That's how our search begins.

However, the illusion dissipates once we complete our education and enter the fast-paced world. We realize the world doesn't recognize us for the love we carry inside. Society has its set of rules. To earn respect, one must work diligently and achieve success.

And let's be honest, society doesn't define success by love, kindness, or peace of mind. It judges you by what you own: the car you drive, the house you live in, the money you make, and the followers you have. In the middle of this, all those fairy tales we heard growing up start to feel fake. We begin to believe the real world only works through currency, reputation, and status.

Humans abandon the very emotion that helps them thrive, love, and start chasing temporary material success. Now, I'm not talking like a priest or an impractical person. I'm simply pointing out the imbalance. Many individuals overlook their emotions and even disregard those who genuinely care for them in their pursuit of material wealth and fleeting desires. They seek to project power and gain validation from others.

When it comes to modern love, the truth is, people want everything, including love, but they would rather not give up anything for it. And maybe you shouldn't have to sacrifice yourself entirely for love. But the fact is, some people do, and when they are abandoned, their belief in love dies. Add to that inflation, rising desires, and endless wants.

People are no longer satisfied with basics. They want luxury, status, and experiences. And love? Love has become merely another task to be completed. Many today searches for a partner only when they feel lonely, not because they truly want to build a life together. That's why globally, many people are dropping the idea of marriage. They feel staying single makes life less stressful. Traveling, partying, and casual sex—for many, these feel more fulfilling than the idea of having a family and raising children.

Family and Marriage: Personal Choices

Having a family or children is a personal choice. But here's my observation: one should only bring a child into this world if they are mentally, physically, and financially ready. Otherwise, bringing a child into suffering is the greatest sin one can commit. Marriage is not solely focused on the wedding day or a social media hashtag.

Marriage requires commitment, companionship, loyalty, friendship, and respect. Remember, a wedding is an event, while marriage is a lifelong commitment between two people. Throughout this journey, you will discover various aspects of your partner's personality, including their moods, anger, and carelessness, yet you will continue to choose them for life. Forgiving and forgetting is what marriage is, and sacrificing and adjusting is what marriage is.

People who are self-centered, impatient, and sensitive should develop an understanding of marriage. Some people think marriage will solve their life problems or cure loneliness, but the fact is, you should be getting married to a person with only one intention: love, acceptance, and commitment.

Anything apart from those qualities isn't marriage; it's gambling. Love is just the first step, but it's these other ingredients that help you survive the long run. I have a friend who was deeply engrossed in a healthy, long-distance relationship. Soon, she wanted to take the next step and ask the guy for marriage.

Professionally, she was thriving. Despite having a decent job and a well-educated background, she turned down a high-paying job offer in another country in Favor of her partner. She prioritized emotions and love above all else.

Months later, she found out that the guy she had been dating for almost a decade was in love with a wealthy single mother. He left my friend and married her instead.

My friend was devastated and depressed, and her primary regret was sacrificing the pay check she could have earned at the new job. Now she is unmarried and single and finding it difficult to settle because she lost faith. The next move feels impossible.

Another friend married a woman in their late thirties. Initially, everything seemed fine. Both were happy; she enjoyed her work, and he was searching for more opportunities for a better life. Then he discovered she was having an affair with her boss.

Later, he discovered that she had married him due to family pressure, a situation faced by many young people in India. Love was sacrificed in the process. There are others who rush into marriage without compatibility or become parents without a financial plan. They struggle, fight, and unintentionally traumatize their children.

When responsibilities take over, love tends to fade away. So, what is more difficult: being in a marriage or becoming parents without preparation? These are the discussions every young person should have before making life-altering choices.

These stories show that love is vital for humans to thrive, but marriage requires more: commitment, friendship, honesty, respect, and independence.

Independence and Responsibility

For women in many countries, managing a career and a child is challenging. Society pressures them to multitask endlessly and be financially independent. Historically, men often disrespected homemakers, and many of them experienced abuse or disappointment, leading women to believe they needed financial independence.

As a woman, I also believe that the most important aspect of life is family and loved ones. But modern complexities have pushed women to seek financial independence. In reality, both genders should share equal responsibility, but sadly, that hasn't been happening much.

That's why single mothers have risen globally; women seek independence first. So be in love; if you have strong values for marriage, do it, but never leave your independence for anyone. And that's the mindset you need to learn.

For men, the primary duty is to look after their family, providing safety, security, and respect. Some men embrace fatherhood and preserve love with their partner, whereas many fail to take accountability, abandoning families due to affairs, alcoholism, or irresponsibility. Such behaviours are the reason why the next generation, often traumatized, rejects the idea of marriage and commitment.

Modern Trends and Global Observations

. In Western countries, many focus on careers until their late thirties, delaying marriage and children.

. In some African countries, couples live together with children without formal marriage.

. LGBTQ+ communities and same-sex marriages have increased, sometimes reducing the emphasis on children.

. Economic pressures, inflation, dating apps, and lack of focus push people away from love and marriage, leading to depression, loneliness, and even suicide.

Why People Lose Faith in Marriage

Commitment and Responsibility: People see parents struggle, perform duties, and complain. They fear losing personal freedom.

Too Many Options: Modern conflicts often lead people to seek strangers online instead of resolving issues with their partner, leading to affairs and broken communication.

Inflation and Lifestyle Pressure: Rising costs, travel, education, and luxury desires create stress and neglect emotional needs. Loneliness cannot be cured with material things.

Independence and Career Focus: In countries like the USA and parts of Europe, young adults focus on careers, casual dating, and personal space. Financial struggles in many households globally push young adults to delay marriage. Even privileged backgrounds don't guarantee bliss. Many pursue freedom and exploration, leaving spouses lonely.

My Take on Marriage

In my twenties, I never wanted to get married. I had preconceived notions, shaped by observation and societal whispers. Today, married to someone I dated, I've realized that even when you think you know a person, marriage reveals entirely new layers.

My advice is to enjoy your twenties, be your own person, and only get married when you're ready to make a lifelong commitment.

Marriage won't feel like a struggle if you choose the right person, someone with whom you can share your daily routine. Maintain realistic expectations. Unrealistic aspirations for a flawless marriage become unfeasible, particularly after becoming a parent. Parenthood changes everything. The responsibility of nurturing and guiding a tiny human being transforms your life. Challenges are daily, relentless, and unlike anything else.

I've been a stage host, a music producer, and an author, but becoming a parent and a mother is, without doubt, the toughest role of all.

Mindset Notes...

1. Be emotionally and financially self-sufficient. Don't burden your partner with your trauma.

2. Marrying or not is your choice, but don't stay in a toxic relationship.

3. Maintain your friendships; they can become anchors when life becomes tough.

4. The greatest treasure is not wealth but a stable love life and family.

5. Real happiness is internal. Don't fake it. Be eternally joyful.

While dating apps may facilitate easy connections, the most challenging task is finding a partner who will be there for you no matter what. Across countries, people seek connection but fear responsibility. Many see casual dating, benching, or situationships as acceptable, avoiding long-term commitment.

As we end this chapter, we've seen the reality—the confusion between economics, finances, marriage, and relationships. Now we need to look more closely at the bigger picture that has caused a divide between men and women for hundreds of years. It's the conditioning passed from generation to generation, shaping ego, inequality, and tension. We can truly rebuild only when we take responsibility and break this pattern, as men and women are equal but have been assigned different duties, which society has complicated.

Break the Myth; Rebuild the Mindset

"Equality is not about gender rights; it's about sharing responsibilities, respect, and opportunities between two genders rightly and equally."

Back in the day, debates circled endlessly around one thing: who ruled the world, men or women? Men were considered the breadwinners, women the homemakers. And with that belief came countless atrocities women faced. Then came the revolution era. In the 1970s, starting in the USA, the feminist movement rose. The message was clear: either you stand for equal rights or you keep the patriarchy alive.

As we transition into the modern era, previously suppressed voices are now audible. We should applaud the people who, through speeches, movements, and art, have challenged the old systems across the globe. Today, men and women need to understand: roles assigned by nature may exist, but human intelligence and potential are shared.

Women are no longer just considered homemakers or "arm candy." Men are no longer mocked for displaying emotions or choosing household responsibilities. We live in a time where anyone can do anything. People have voices. Men, too, have discovered new sides of themselves, qualities women appreciate and society once shamed them for.

Today, we celebrate LGBTQ+ identities and accept the choices people make. Therefore, if you continue to engage in debates and suppress the voices of those of the opposite gender, you are only creating more division within yourself.

This is the era of building together with different minds and perspectives, not just male and female. The wise will understands. The immature will keep debating.

The Weight of Stereotypes

Have you ever witnessed someone roll their eyes when you, as a woman, made a sharp comment in a conference room?

Have you ever seen men react with shock when you discuss period pain in a serious, non-joking manner?

Or do women express surprise when men say they love cooking, as if recipes and Is food something alien for men? That's how deep stereotypes run.

Men statistically crash cars more often, yet women are still called the crazy drivers. Entire professions—pilots, surgeons, and CEOs—still treat women as outsiders. And no matter how qualified, women are often taken less seriously.

On the other hand, men are crowned fearless. But the truth is, many avoid conflict, and many walk away from fights. And that's perfectly acceptable. Fear is not a sign of weakness; it's a fundamental aspect of being human.

Society has simply assigned it different meanings based on gender. Household chores shouldn't be gendered. Yet people treat it as a big deal when a man does laundry or changes a diaper. Being domestic isn't feminine; it's human.

Here's another truth:

A man's journey can be equally challenging, especially without financial power. The moment he loses his job or fails to provide; society treats him as incomplete. That doesn't seem right. Respect isn't gendered. It's a human right.

- A man is still a man, even if he's broke.
- A woman is still a woman even if she chooses not to cook or have children.

If we truly want equality, we must respect people, their emotions, opinions, and work, without judgment. It's not just about empowering women. It's also about freeing men from the pressure to always provide, always lead, and always hold it in. Equality is two-way support. That's the only way forward. Men and women can thrive together. Yes, men may need to step up more since they still dominate the workforce in most places. Men can pave the way to equality, not with insecurity but with grace.

Women should come together in support of one another. It's important to avoid competition and instead focus on uplifting each other.

. Let women laugh loud.
. Let men enjoy skincare.
. Let men gossip.
. Let women lead.
. Let both genders take space unapologetically.
. Let's make being human normal again.

A Personal Note on Stereotypes

I've lived this. I've been taken lightly, dismissed, and judged not because I was wrong, but because I had the nerve to speak up. I've been told that my intelligence is too much, and it was intended as an insult. But I'm not trying to intimidate anyone. I have a clear perspective, and I express it honestly.

It unnerves some individuals, particularly those who feel invincible in the face of challenge. Still, I'm lucky. I've had incredible male friends who've supported me, guided me, and treated me as an equal.

But let's not sugarcoat the truth: in most homes, most careers, and most marriages, it's women who are still expected to compromise. Men often have smoother roads not because they asked, but because the world built it that way.

It is time for us to stop paving the familiar roads of the past and to begin constructing a new path that is equitable for all.

The Illusion of Equality Starts at Home

The world has always been divided mostly into two visible genders: male and female. For generations, we've coexisted, not just as humans but across species. From the moment we're born, nature provides us with identity. Then society takes over. It names us, shapes us, and cages us.

We grow up under invisible rules. We're told what to become, how to act, and who to be. And we follow because that's how it has always been. However, as soon as you venture into the real world, your illusions crumble. You see people with unimaginable beauty, confidence, courage, and power.

And your mind begins to question:

. Who decided our roles?

. Who said a woman must be soft and a man must be strong? Let me tell you some stories.

Story: Sid and Maggie

Sid and **Maggie** were siblings raised in the same house.

Sid was a nomad, free-spirited and uninterested in rules or routines. Maggie was ambitious, razor-sharp, and driven to succeed. Their father ran a flourishing business across countries. But when retirement came, guess who he picked to carry the legacy?

Sid—the wanderer. Maggie, having completed her MBA and possessing a clear understanding of the business's future, found herself overlooked. Her ambition was labelled arrogance. Her confidence? Manipulative. Her clarity was perceived as a threat. Sid's disinterest was excused as charm. Maggie's hunger was mistaken for cunning. Women aren't denied because they're incapable. They're denied because they were never expected to lead.

Story: Sara

Sara was an only child. Her father was an alcoholic who abused her mother regularly. From childhood, she saw destruction. Her father never once treated her like a daughter. He hurled abuse at her, ignored her, and rejected her femininity. That trauma ran so deep that Sara slowly stopped identifying as a girl. She began seeing herself as the man she wished existed in her home.

She wanted to protect, provide, and lead. Eventually, she found love in women, and it made sense. She wasn't confused. She was just trying to become the person her father never was. She became the protector she had always needed.

Sara once married a man to make her parents content. But even now, she hides who she really is. The shame is not hers; it's societies.

Story: Alex and Priti

Alex was a chef. **Priti** was a banker. Both were working professionals. One day, Priti was promoted and offered a transfer abroad. She was thrilled but unsure if Alex would support her. Upon hearing the news, Alex found himself torn between celebrating Priti's success and feeling apprehensive about disrupting his life. After contemplation, he boldly decided to relocate alongside her, secure new employment, and champion her aspirations.

Years later, when Priti became pregnant, she took a sabbatical break, and in the meantime, Alex advanced in his career. Men like Alex are the reason women like Priti thrive, and they are also why marriages work. He didn't allow pride or ego to interfere. They both understood their relationship, priorities, and roles when necessary. The world is only complete when both genders rise together without diminishing each other.

Gender Inequality

Global Glimpses In some countries, suppression is subtle. In others, it's loud and brutal. Women were not allowed to drive in Saudi Arabia until recently. In many Islamic states, women still need a man's permission to travel, to work, and to live.

In America, a country the world looks up to, women had to march, fight, and protest just to work, vote, and build a life outside the kitchen. In Bollywood and Hollywood, men still earn five times more than women for the same screen time. Tom Cruise makes 100 million dollars. Cameron Diaz receives 20 million dollars. Oppression wears many clothes. Occasionally, it's the law. Occasionally, it's silence at the dinner table.

Rethinking Masculinity and Femininity

Masculinity isn't about being loud, dominant, or emotionless. True masculinity is when you make others feel safe. It's not about controlling; it's about protecting without making others feel small. Femininity isn't weakness. It's not about cooking, cleaning, or being soft-spoken. True femininity is nurturing with strength. It's when a woman builds, balances, and blossoms all at once. Let's stop boxing people.

Let men cry. Let women lead. Let girls raise their voices. Let boys talk about fear.

The Everyday Inequality

Let's say a man and a woman both work 9 to 5. They come home. One changes clothes, sits down, and watches TV. The other enters the kitchen. Guess who does what? The burden of housework, parenting, and emotional labour still falls on women even when both partners work the same hours.

And the world calls this normal. Inequality doesn't just sit in boardrooms. It cooks in kitchens and hides in silence. This is where inequality truly lives, not just in offices, but in bedrooms, kitchens, and quiet compromises.

We live in a world where gender roles are breaking, but mindsets need to catch up. Let men wear jewelry. Let women race Formula 1. Let people choose their lives without shame. The only thing that needs fixing is our outdated perspective.

The Purpose

The reason this chapter arrived at me is simple: as we grow and play our part in as a society, it is important that whenever we emerge, we bring a fresh approach. We must broaden our perspective, regardless of the influence or conditioning we have received. We have for too long tied rejection and validation to fragile egos, even in love and relationships.

Men often perceive rejection as a blow to their self-esteem. But does hearing a "no" truly silence your heart? And for women, does validation from a man really make your life complete overnight? We must break this pattern. Encourage each other, colleague, friend, and co-worker. Respect each other's no. Human capability, passion, and talent often go unnoticed due to personal baggage, as demonstrated by movements like #MeToo. Those who exploit are only feeding their egos by crushing another's self-respect. That is not strength; that is weakness.

Therefore, when you receive the chance in your life, take it. Build a safer community for generations to come. Shape thoughts. Encourage progressive perspectives. Break the old provocative ideas about gender roles and inequality. If you're young and have the chance to break the patterns established by previous generations.

Remember this:

. Avoid viewing individuals of the opposite gender as a threat and instead collaborate as a team.

. Don't put others in compromising situations.

. Respect the no when it's said.

The world is complete only when both genders fulfil their roles without making the other feel small. Suppression is for the weak-minded. Empowerment is for the wise.

Mindset Notes...

1. List the thoughts you hold about the opposite gender. Then share them openly. Notice where you are right and where you may be carrying bias.

2. Write down the things you were told about the opposite gender while growing up. Compare them with reality and the changes you now see. Journaling these reflections can help you reshape your perception.

As we close this hard-hitting chapter on gender myths and equality, we now step into one that is far more practical and just as deep.

People often confuse creativity and progress with simply following patterns, trends, and the need to belong to a club. People rarely think creatively, and those who do often face doubts, questions, and mockery.

There is also a certain invisible race, a race of beauty, fame, and validation, where thoughts are crafted and truth is suppressed with ease. and beautification is encouraged even when everything inside is hollow.

However, it is important to remember that history is shaped by individuals who challenge the status quo, not by those who heedlessly follow the crowd.

Only Dead Fish Go with the Flow

"The more you follow the crowd, the less visible you become to yourself."

The generation to which you currently belong, my dear, is an unusual one, a world characterized by numerous contradictions. On one hand there is advancement and convenience: life at your fingertips. You can order food, learn a skill, or speak to someone halfway across the world in seconds.

On the other hand, we have become restless, anxious, and distracted. There is curiosity about creating something meaningful, but the grip on execution is slipping. The mind keeps wandering. And when shallow inspiration piles up, it breeds a culture of borrowed dreams and fake confidence.

I remember when I was struggling to build a niche. I kept scrolling through social media, searching for ideas, searching for my interest. Then I saw a long-lost friend's social media account. It looked impressive, engaging, and successful. She was a travel influencer. At that moment I felt inspired. I started planning my path, convinced I would begin the next day.

But the next day never came. I woke up at noon, drained from staying up all night. By then the fire was gone and the plans were forgotten. That night, the same cycle repeats. The endless scroll steals your time, shapes your thoughts, and dictates who you want to be and how you see success. That is where pseudo-inspiration sneaks in.

The Pseudo-Inspiration Trap

People are wasting their most precious years on social media and chasing trends. They can recall a viral TikTok dance instantly, but ask them about their country or a historical figure and they will fall flat. Instead of learning from real stories, they follow actors, singers, and influencers hiding behind carefully staged images. These idols glamorize drugs, casual relationships, and self-destruction.

Masculinity is reduced to aggression. Femininity is reduced to manipulation. And the media broadcasts what sells, not what heals. No wonder, even with all the possibilities, people still feel hollow. Celebrities do not owe responsibility to followers. They are simply making money.

You see them in luxury cars and designer clothes, but you have only seen a fraction of their reality. Behind the scenes, many do unethical things to survive. Fans will not see it, yet they still defend them. Why do we argue in the comment section with people who do not even recognize us, while disregarding our own peace?

I remember when trends and viral fashion made me a shopaholic. I was consuming ads and spending enormous amounts on clothes. Eventually I understood that while human needs are limited, desires are boundless. I realized that the game is fundamentally commercial and we frequently fall victim to it.

Reflect:

Am I engaging in this activity because it aligns with my true desires, or merely because it is what everyone else is doing? Your bills, your peace, and your dreams—none of them will be paid by herd mentality, trends, or followers. It is you. Avoid being manipulated. Those who genuinely succeed don't feel the need to display their achievements. They create quietly and authentically.

Your mind will constantly push you to chase borrowed dreams. It will make you feel directionless, constantly thinking, "If I chose the same path, I would achieve equal success." But that is a lie. Only by looking within, giving yourself time, and discovering your strengths can you stay away from the herd.

The Herd Mentality

Herd mentality is not new. While growing up, I observed that my neighbours would copy each other by buying items that others purchased, even if they could not afford them. Today social media has intensified the phenomenon. People open their feeds every day and instantly feel they want something even when they do not. Purchasing an iPhone on EMI with limited income or spending $500 on a concert solely to share a selfie exemplifies the prevalent herd mentality.

Many will not admit they borrowed or begged for it. Those who truly understand money rarely waste it proving a point. Even influencers often barter visibility with brands. Behind the image, it is survival. Herd mentality has always existed. The only difference now is that the internet amplifies it. Trends are dressed up as movements, and people proudly wear borrowed identities.

The Illusion of Beauty and Fame

Famous personalities set beauty standards, and young girls bear the consequences. Surgery is replacing natural beauty. People hesitate to show their natural faces. When someone does, they are criticized. Everyone criticizes plastic beauty, yet natural beauty increasingly looks alien to a generation raised on airbrushed faces.

In South Korea, many women consider undergoing surgery to be a normal practice before they enter the workforce. If this mindset spreads, individuals around the world may feel pressured to conform, even at the expense of their health. From Hollywood to Bollywood, all we consume is the same pattern of looking successful.

We have sold the idea that looking attractive through beautification surgeries, branded clothes, perfect aesthetics, and traveling the world equals a picture-perfect life. Have we ever considered how lonely or depressed many of these individuals might be? Despite their unstable marriages and children raised in different households, we continue to feel envious, convinced they are leading perfect lives.

What you see is just the highlight reel, not reality. Beauty fades with time. What stays intact is your persona. It will be remembered even when you are gone. Stop nourishing only external beauty. Focus on your internal one.

Life, Responsibility, and Your Fire

Some of you are carrying responsibilities far earlier than you should. Maybe you have lost a parent. Maybe you are facing financial or personal crises. If you cannot chase your desires immediately because duty calls first, you are still on the right path. Some legends hustled through their twenties and lived freely in their thirties and years after. Your time will come. Maintain your faith. Carry your fire.

Posting your delicious meal on social media is not real success. Feeling happy on social media is not fulfilment. Buying followers to appear desirable is not popularity. Becoming a parent influencer while spending limited time with your children is a false achievement. Today people lecture or make reels about current affairs, entertainment, spiritual knowledge, and astrology, but they fail to make real human connections.

Ask yourself

What are your best moments? The answer will be the ones that are not captured on your phone. Never suppress your capabilities. Always take risks. Never confuse someone else's highlight reel with your life's blueprint. Trends fade. Viral moments die. But the fire you build inside is what endures.

If no one offers you a seat at their table, build your own. If you cannot afford something, do not cripple your future to pretend you are rich. Put your life first. Build wealth the right way.

You are not behind. That perception is simply a reflection of the excitement surrounding your early years. Believe me, you have time. The world will move at its pace whether you follow it or not. Many are standing on the side of the road trying to sell you something—products, ideas, or agendas. It is up to you to understand that not everything you see and hear is true.

The Era of Controlled Narratives

We live in a world where anyone can sell or influence anything. Make enough noise, and people hand you, their attention. Every generation had its obsessions—pop culture, ads, music—but we were not trapped in it. Now, with AI creeping into everything, illusions will only deepen. Deepfake videos of world leaders, celebrity endorsements, or fabricated incidents—millions will believe them.

Future kids may talk more to robots than to humans. They may forget how to feel something real. The youth are the easiest targets. Songs, films, and influencers sell drugs, promote casual sex, and showcase fake lifestyles, convincing young people that they are missing out. Ads do the same. One side says, "Say no to drugs," while the other glamorizes smoking or drinking. Society now calls parties incomplete without alcohol.

History Repeats in New Costumes

Initially the media painted Hitler as simple, disciplined, and even kind. People believed it. But once power was in his hands, the world saw one of history's most ruthless dictators. That is the power of controlled narratives: they turn monsters into saints and sell lies as truth.

And it is still happening. Celebrities promote junk while pretending to care about health. Influencers endorse alcohol they do not even drink.

If you think you are safe, think again. Spectators are the easiest to control. Remain silent for too long, and you may fail to realize when you are being manipulated, exploited, and ultimately discarded. The world will not change. The media will not stop lying. But you can change yourself. Maybe it will not shake their empire, but it will change your life.

Only dead fish go with the flow.

Nobody should dictate how you live, love, dress, or decorate your home. Copying others leads to losing your sense of self. Start by understanding who you are. Only then can you confront the world and its distractions and noise. Entertainment is fine; just do not drown in it. Occasionally challenge the norm. It is easy to follow. It is rare to think.

Remember the things that seem free. They cost you your focus. In today's world, focus is the most expensive thing you can buy. Either you control your attention or they will. The world will tell you to stay busy, stay ahead, and follow trends. But only those who are truly dedicated to their work can adapt. And you, you are alive.

Mindset Notes...

1. Control your digital diet. Set timings for digital consumption. Do not create accounts on every platform. Buzz off, notifications.

2. Promote and practice sustainability. Wear repeated clothes proudly. Create a trend of sustainability rather than random shopping.

3. Use social media for growth. Create blogs, sell, buy, and connect. Use it for your benefit and that of others, not just as a distraction.

4. Think independently. Do not chase everything you see online. Pause. Reflect. Ask, does this material make sense for me? Learn to think for yourself.

If you have reached this far and completed this chapter, pause and realize how often we are flowing in a world that is artificial and mostly limited to the virtual. Trends and virality may look harmless, but they block real progress and creativity while also giving rise to unseen, damaging emotions. These emotions, if left unchecked, can quietly eat away at us. That is why the next chapter is so important.

A young mind does not just need intelligence to build and create; it needs emotional intelligence to balance, to stay kind, and to be empathetic. In a world growing more competitive and judgmental each day, what will truly make you thrive is not envy, but the ability to understand more and react less.

Emotionally Intelligent, Not Emotionally Exhausted

"People often believe IQ is the key to success, but the truth is that 80% of your life is shaped not by IQ but by EQ, or emotional intelligence".

We don't lose people because of situations or conflicts. We lose them because, instead of responding, we reacted. Have you ever lost a friend or loved one because of your mood? Perhaps you were experiencing anger, anxiety, or overwhelm, which led you to say something you did not intend. That is where emotional intelligence steps in. It is the silent skill that either saves or destroys our relationships, peace, and self-worth.

You are not truly fortunate simply because you possess money, fame, or love. True fortune lies in cultivating mindfulness, empathy, wisdom, and inner peace. You do not need logic to feel emotions, but you urgently require it to handle them. Without it, you will stay stuck in the same emotional loops.

Life will throw challenges, heartbreaks, and struggles, and often, in those moments, we lose good people. Most emotional reactions are temporary. Unfortunately, the damage they cause is often permanent.

This era requires individuals to cultivate emotional intelligence to sustain themselves. As you have learned in earlier chapters, the alarming issues our generation faces today ripple over to future generations.

Every advancement shifts mindsets. The more comfortable and facilitated we become, the more ignorant we risk becoming. With the overconsumption of social media, dating apps, artificial food, and endless exposure, society is losing its core: human connection. Bonds are breaking. People are becoming self-centered, opportunistic, and unwilling to share.

But here is the truth:

Humans are the only species gifted with both intellect and emotions. We are meant to connect. The happiest moments in life do not come from what we cling to but from what we share. And sharing is not just about wealth.

It involves providing a support system, a heart that embraces imperfections, and a mind that lessens judgment and increases understanding. That is what makes a human complete. Yet today ego is on the rise. Insecurities are spreading. People are pulling each other down instead of lifting each other up.

Nobody has ever achieved anything alone. There has always been a team, a supporter, and a helping hand. Forgetting this truth means forgetting humanity itself. In the race for followers, trends, comparisons, and fake praise, life is becoming unnecessarily complex.

People whose egos feed only on attention and validation are multiplying, and even those with emotional intelligence struggle to express it. They are mocked, harassed, or silenced until they, too, give up and join the ignorant club. That is the power of bitterness. It spreads like poison. Look around.

Society is suffocating with fake validation, unhealed trauma, and hypocrisy. Children are not receiving proper affection because parents are overworked, drowning in debt, and distracted. Restless scrolling keeps people anxious. Broken families leave scars. Odd working hours damage both mind and body. People are going numb and losing direction and balance.

And if so, much chaos surrounds us, how do you expect emotionally intelligent people to grow? That is why cultivating emotional intelligence has never been more urgent. If it is learned early in life, it benefits not just the individual but the entire society. This world desperately needs not just smarter people but also kinder, more empathetic human beings.

My Personal Experience

The reason I strongly believe in emotional intelligence is because of what I have seen in my life. I have met people who, in the heat of anger, would cross boundaries. Others lived in hypocrisy yet were adamant about never accepting their faults.

Some constantly sought attention. Somehow, I always thought differently. I never felt the need to boast or draw attention to myself. I was the first to reach out to a lonely person, the one who naturally empathized with others. I retaliated, but mostly in self-defense.

I have had heated moments too. Looking back, though, I realize one of my greatest mistakes was defending myself too much. I explained, argued, and justified endlessly to people who never cared, to people who never changed.

Some grow older but not wiser. Over the years, I have given chances to people, and I have learned a difficult truth: those who truly care will never repeatedly cross boundaries. If someone does, emotional intelligence means knowing when to walk away and letting them heal on their own.

After meeting so many wrong people, I have reached a conclusion: if you are not emotionally intelligent, the world will label you an emotional fool. That is why emotional intelligence is not optional. It is survival in today's world.

What Is Emotional Intelligence?

Please set aside the textbook definitions. Here is mine: An emotionally intelligent person knows how to listen before judging or reacting. They understand their emotions first before trying to understand someone else. They ask themselves, "What if I were in their place?" instead of reacting blindly. They listen more. They empathize. They do not rush to conclusions. There is a saying: "To understand the world, first understand yourself." Your triggers. Your values. Your pain. Your desires. You are a world within.

Once you dive into yourself, the fog starts to clear. You begin to respond, not react. You make better choices. You live with more clarity. Yes, it is challenging, particularly during youth, when there is considerable pressure, noise, and uncertainty. But that is when emotional intelligence matters the most.

Real-Life Example: Mia

Mia was the heart of every gathering–kind, accommodating, and soft-spoken. She would show up when you needed her, make people laugh, and offer support without being asked. But there was another side to her.

When things did not go her way, or when her efforts were not acknowledged, she became bitter. She lashed out, kept score, and blamed others for her pain. In anger, she spoke harshly, weaponized her kindness, and forgot the relationships she once cherished.

Because of this, Mia began losing friends. Some tried to help her. She could see the problem, but her ego stood in the way. She rarely apologized, and when she did, the same pattern repeated. She could not stand it when others were upset or distant. She immediately started a fight, taunted, or shut down. She used people when she needed them and vanished when they needed her.

You can argue with people, but not with their ego, rigid thoughts, or adamant attitudes; it's a waste of time. If you have ever met someone like Mia, you know how draining it feels.

People like this often appear narcissistic. They are hyper-aware of others' flaws while blind to their own. They reject accountability, repeat mistakes, and blame others. A narcissist constantly seeks attention, yearning for control, validation, and emotional dominance.

They clash with emotionally intelligent people because emotional intelligence does not feed egos; it reflects truth. Yes, trauma shapes us, but accountability matters. Your pain is yours alone, and no one deserves your behaviour just because you have suffered.

Prioritizing your peace isn't selfish, and some people need to confront those they blame for their trauma instead of receiving kindness. These people need kindness, but not the enabling kind. They need someone who helps them see that the world is not responsible for their healing. Therapy, reflection, or simply honest effort can help, but without emotional intelligence, their emotions harm more than they heals.

The Power of Emotional Intelligence Ruben vs. The CEO—Two Faces of Emotional Intelligence

Ruben's Story:

Ruben, a young corporate professional, often belittles his juniors due to his behaviour and position. In the corporate world, we frequently hear stories about individuals who overshadow their team members, who equally contribute to creating success stories. While people like Ruben may formally acknowledge others by mentioning their names or offering praise, they often convey that their achievements are solely dependent on their own efforts, undermining the contributions of their colleagues.

Their behaviours create friction and often force people to leave the workplace. Toxicity is rising in these environments because leaders must have both logical and empathetic intelligence.

The CEO's Story

In contrast, a food delivery app's CEO noticed that his delivery staff had gone on strike, demanding fair wages. Instead of ignoring them, he dressed like them for a day and delivered food himself. Only then did he grasp the exhaustion, the stress, and the struggle. He raised wages, added bonuses, and improved working conditions.

This was not fiction. Similar stories have happened, like the founder of Zomato in India. That is emotional intelligence. That is empathy in leadership. Professionally, emotionally intelligent leaders do not just create profits. They change lives. Personally, emotionally intelligent partners sustain relationships, while emotionally immature couples often collapse under pressure. If you cannot understand yourself, you will never truly understand another person.

Therefore, creating a healthy space and fostering respect are essential in every relationship so that individuals can understand each other and grow. How to Become Emotionally Intelligent Knowledge is gained, but wisdom is acquired when it is applied. Emotional intelligence, like any skill, takes practice.

Life is chaotic: deadlines, traffic, misunderstandings, and endless noise. Amid all this, how do you protect your calm?

. Start by slowing down.

. Breathe. Pause before reacting.

. Not every taunt, trigger, or drama deserves your energy.

Meditation and Reading: The Only Two Tools You Need

Any form of exercise that aligns your body or mind, whether it's yoga or meditation, can clear your mind, soften your reactions, and sharpen your decisions. Meditation doesn't only mean sitting cross-legged; it can also include activities like cooking, painting, walking, or even listening to music. Anything that helps anchor you in the present moment can be considered a form of meditation.

Reading, the most underrated superpower, heals anxiety, sharpens empathy, and quiets your mind. Books offer you the wisdom of others without living their pain. Reading makes you reflect, imagine, and empathize, and in doing so, you build emotional depth.

I say these words as someone who lived in anxiety, always worrying about the future. Only when I embraced meditation and reading did I gain clarity and confidence. Watching short videos, reels, or any form of social media only increases anxiety. To balance this, one must pick up a book and read at least three or four pages a day.

When you become emotionally intelligent, you will:

. Place yourself in fewer messy situations.

. Avoid emotional self-harm

. Respond with grace

. Stop chasing validation from people who do not value you. Learn to observe without absorbing.

What Emotional Intelligence Really Looks Like It is not about being calm 24/7. It is about:

. Understanding and managing your emotions

. Respond instead of reacting.

. Setting healthy boundaries

. Listening without judgment

. Saying no without guilt

. Living with presence and gratitude

Emotional Wisdom in Action Quick reactions, gossip-driven opinions, and mood-based decisions destroy friendships, partnerships, and careers. In life, your relationships define you. Do not lose them to ego or pride.

Start practicing:

. Gratitude for small joys

. Self-love on challenging days

. Pausing before reacting

. Walking away from drama

. Speaking with intention

. Saying no with grace

Mindset Notes...

1. When was the last time you made a choice based on your mood? How did it turn out?

2. Have you ever judged someone before hearing their full story?

3. What is one relationship you deeply value, and are you doing enough to protect it? Emotional intelligence is not about avoiding emotions. It is about understanding them so they do not control you.

As we complete this chapter and understand how regulating emotions can take you a long way, making you more aware of both situations and people, we realize that awareness and acceptance are the true foundations of growth. But growth does not happen in isolation.

The people around you influence your thoughts, your choices, and even the way you see yourself. The right tribe can shape you into your best self, while the wrong one can silently drag you backward and make life far more difficult. In the next chapter, we will explore this powerful truth: how your circle defines your direction.

Not All Are Your Friends: Guard Your Circle, Choose Your Table

"You are the culmination of the individuals you welcome into your life."

The earlier you realize the importance of your tribe; the sooner you can say goodbye to a lot of drama in your life. Surround yourself with people who align with your mindset; they will feed your brain with positivity and strength. When I was growing up, my father would always tell us to choose our friends wisely. He would say, "Always sit at tables where the conversations are about growth, ideas, and wisdom." At the time I was too young to grasp what he truly meant.

I believed in equality, considered everyone a friend, and never made distinctions. Years later, I finally understand what he was trying to tell us, now that I stand at a point in life where I have the wisdom to write this book.

The Influence of Your Circle

When we are young, we tend to see people only for what's on the surface. We are naïve, curious, and still figuring out life, with little understanding of how people can shape us. Anyone who talks kindly, helps us out, or shares a laugh becomes important. Many of us are gullible and vulnerable.

We hold the belief that everyone is our friend and open our hearts to those who bring us comfort. We collect different kinds of friends—travel buddies, office colleagues, schoolmates, neighbours—but the rarest of them all are those precious few who genuinely influence the course of our lives.

Psychology says you become like the people you spend the most time with, and it's true. The more time you spend with wise, diligent, and productive people, the more you become like them. On the flip side, if you are constantly surrounded by drifters, gossip-mongers, or bitter people who blame life and others for everything, you will unknowingly absorb those traits too. It happens subtly, without you even realizing it.

Two Types of People

There are two types of people in this world: Those who have the power to influence others. Those who allow themselves to be influenced. If you're in the first group, you will notice people around you adopting your habits, words, and attitude. You will see them repeating your phrases, dressing like you, and mirroring your lifestyle. And you will not feel threatened, because when you're secure in yourself, you naturally want others to grow too.

But occasionally you might become irritated when someone imitates you without admitting it. Realize this quickly—those are not your friends; they are silently competing with you. If you fall into the second category of being influenced, it is important to exercise caution.

Life introduces you to all kinds of people. If you spend too much time with those who are pessimistic, bitter, insecure, or reckless, you will start adopting their mindset and habits.

Teenagers and people in their early twenties often experience pressure to conform to group norms to avoid exclusion. They adopt the habits of a few friends without knowing whether they will help or harm them. Social media and the idols they follow often influence these choices. That is why people say, Choose your idol wisely.

What You Can and Can't Choose

Some things in life you don't get to choose, like your parents, your family, or the place you're born. They're attached to you by destiny. If you have a loving, supportive family, you're fortunate. If not, you'll have to fight your battles the hard way. But friendships are different. That's the one relationship you are free to pick for yourself, and it's beautiful because it comes without conditions. Good friends won't demand that you change or meet unrealistic expectations. They will accept you as you are and still inspire you to become better.

I firmly believe that people blessed with exceptional friendships are among the wealthiest on the planet. Even one trustworthy friend is enough to light up your world—someone you can laugh with, cry to, and share your life's journey with. Sadly, in today's world, genuine friendships have become rare. People have grown insecure and competitive.

Many wear smiles in front of you and frown the moment you turn your back. Some shower you with praise while secretly hoping for your downfall. If you notice such energy, it's wise to adjust your environment promptly. Don't wait for multiple signs. The people you surround yourself with during your growing years silently shape your future.

The Story of Distressed Veronica

Veronica was in her late twenties. All her life she had been stern, strong-headed, and opinionated. She had many relationships in the past, but this time she was serious and ready to take it further. Veronica had one flaw: she was short-tempered. Perhaps this was why her love life was never stable.

One morning she received a text from her boyfriend saying he was leaving her and getting married that same day. Shocked, anxious, and in tears, she dialled his number countless times, desperate for closure. Months earlier Veronica's sister had warned her about this man, sensing something was wrong.

But Veronica was in denial. She fought with her sister, furious at her "interference." After he got married, her boyfriend still agreed to meet her. Veronica thought this was a way to keep the relationship alive. It was her biggest mistake. She would spend the day with him, but in the evening, he would go back to his wife. Jealousy and anger consumed her.

Instead of turning to her sister for emotional support, she drifted toward a group of friends who told her the only way to cope with such feelings was through substances. They said, "Take a chill pill," and introduced her to weed and cocaine. These friends didn't offer guidance; instead, they merely distracted her.

Over time, she became addicted and increasingly aggressive, often taking her frustrations out on her family. She spent five years entangled in this complicated relationship. Then, one day, she uncovered the truth: after five years filled with deception, he revealed that he was about to become a father, all while still giving her false hopes of a potential "rebound." That moment shattered her illusions. She realized how much time she had wasted—both on him and on the wrong set of friends who encouraged destructive habits instead of helping her heal.

Veronica was susceptible to influence, and her selection of friends resulted in significant consequences. The lesson: Veronica's story shows that heartbreak, betrayal, and misery are part of growing up.

However, having a solid support system is crucial. Her ignorance and arrogance blinded her from understanding her sister's perspective. She chose the wrong circle, which introduced her to escapism rather than teaching her to face the storm with strength. She wasted her precious years and damaged her health.

Remember, genuine friends will always act as your mirror; they will encourage you to move on and face the trouble instead of escaping from it.

The Story of Novan

Novan, in his early twenties, came from a small city with big dreams. His family was large and financially struggling. His limited education deprived him of many opportunities. But Novan was hardworking, restless, passionate, and curious. He moved to the city in search of work, willing to take any job. All he wanted was the right set of people to recognize his potential and offer him an opportunity. He observed, learned, and adapted.

He noticed the difference between successful people and mediocre ones. He learned the power of dressing well, communicating, and maintaining positive body language. He accepted a lower-paying job at a large company, motivated by the opportunity to learn in a dynamic environment.

During his spare time, he attended seminars and read books he discovered in the office, while deliberately avoiding idle conversations at home. Gradually his dedication paid off. He got noticed, earned an internship at a multinational company, and eventually secured a permanent role.

Novan worked diligently, learned on the job, and grew his skills. He achieved reputation, financial stability, and most importantly, wisdom. He understood early on that surrounding yourself with genuine, positive, and skilled people makes success inevitable.

Two Lives, Two Outcomes

Veronica's and Novan's lives both show the power of your tribe. One fell into destructive habits that took years to escape. The other surrounded himself with growth-minded people and flourished. Your circle can either be the rope that pulls you out or the chain that drags you down.

My Personal Note on Friendship

Be friends with whoever you want, but know your boundaries. Respect everyone, but protect your mindset. Some people look great, speak eloquently, and appear to have it all, but the company they keep reveals their character.

A person is known by the company they keep. I've seen manipulative friendships where one person surrounds themselves with less confident people who call them friends but treat them like assistants, just so that person can feel powerful. I've also seen humble friendships where growth and respect flow both ways. The difference? One is built on control. The other is built on genuine care.

Social Media and Friendship

Most of you have grown up with social media; it's become a big part of life. It's an effortless platform to make friends, and I won't criticize it completely. After all, some of us have genuinely found friends here. Some have even found life partners. But friendship is a treasure you need to cultivate and maintain. Social media can be a dynamic environment.

Online friends mostly show achievements and joyful pictures, but the real test of friendship is in a crisis. The ones who show up in person are your true friends. Stop taking social media so-called friends too seriously. Don't let their opinions disrupt your tranquility. If a comment from an online friend makes you anxious or depressed, pause. True friends guide you right and make the effort to connect offline. Focus on them.

Mindset Notes...

1. Who are the five people I spend the most time with?

2. Do they inspire growth or enable my worst habits?

3. Which friendships feel heavy or transactional?

4. Who genuinely shows up when it matters? Friendship shouldn't be a delicate matter.

True friendship is your chosen family. Seek people who match your mindset and accept your thoughts, outfits, and background, and spend time only with those who do. Your tribe is vital; they shape your mindset, fuel your ambitions, and leave their mark on your hardest days. But practically speaking, not everyone is lucky enough to discover their tribe early in life. It takes time, phases, and constant meetings with new people.

That is why the next chapter is written to guide you: to ensure you never end up in a place where you can't set boundaries. Always test the people who really want to be in your life. Learn to protect your space, your energy, and most importantly, the two most powerful letters of your life: NO.

The Power of Saying No

"You are the solo rider of your life. No matter how much love you provide, people will always prioritize themselves. That is why you must choose yourself first. The sooner you realize this, the more you will save yourself from heartbreak and unrealistic expectations."

No matter where you are born, across continents and cultures, there is a strange conditioning almost all of us grow up with: people expect you to say yes. Yes, it makes you polite, acceptable, and easy to like. But the moment you say no, suddenly you are rude, arrogant, selfish, or difficult. People, innocent and naïve, end up complicating their lives by saying yes when deep inside they wanted to scream no. They say yes to avoid judgment, conflict, and disappointment with someone. But at what cost? Every false yes is a betrayal of your truth.

No is not taboo.

It is not wrong to say no. It is not offensive, selfish, or outdated. What is wrong is abandoning yourself just to make others comfortable. What is wrong is erasing your voice in the name of being kind. Learn to pause and listen to yourself before giving an answer. If the answer is no, say it calmly, respectfully, and clearly. Set your boundaries. Keep your intentions honest. You are not selfish. You are simply done being the yes person everywhere.

"No" is a full sentence.

You Can't Make Everyone Happy: Humans are wired to seek approval. A toddler feels proud when praised. A young woman feels validated when complimented. A man feels important when his boss appreciates him. Validation feels beneficial because it feeds us. But prioritizing the happiness of others often means neglecting your own needs.

. You hand others the power to control you.

. You create a trap for yourself.

My Internship Lesson

In my early twenties, during an internship, I had a colleague whom people often described as aloof. One day, I decided to ask him about the rumours. He smiled faintly. "They call me those names because I don't entertain them. They might be my coworkers, but we aren't like-minded.

Being with them would mean saying yes to things I don't want. I'm not here to please everyone." I asked, "Didn't that cost you job opportunities?" He leaned back calmly. "On the contrary, it actually helped me secure a job." During my interview, I said no to offers that didn't align with me. The boss respected it. He said, 'You're difficult to convince. That clarity is precisely what I need.'" That day I understood something important. Saying no is humility. It is awareness of what you want in life.

Start saying no where it matters.

. Decline the weekend office party you dislike.

. Avoid actions that don't match your identity, even if others think they're trendy.

. Say no to addictions or unhealthy habits just to fit in.

. Say no to overspending, even if you have money, because you are saving for something meaningful. Break the pattern. Notice how people respond to your boundaries.

The people who respect them deserve a place in your life.

Ross: The Guy Who Doesn't Play the Game

Ross, a sharp and grounded guy in his mid-twenties, gives his best every day in a fast-paced marketing firm. Everyone around him wants to rise quickly and is willing to do anything to please seniors, from coffee runs to endless flattery.

Ross is unbothered. He believes in results, not performance. Others rise through people-pleasing, but he stays focused. He keeps learning, improving himself, and applying for opportunities where real work is valued. Ross knows there is a place where contribution matters more than fake praise. He is walking his path without selling himself in the process.

The Social Media Frenzy

We all live dual lives, one offline and one online. People judge you even if you don't reply immediately. Promotions, proposals, and opportunities often depend on how fast you respond. Fragile egos measure your worth by your availability.

Many attend unwanted Zoom calls or group meetings because they are scared to refuse. Saying no has become a big deal. You are expected to justify it. But sometimes "I don't feel like it" is reason enough.

Stop being too available

Your availability will be taken for granted. Know your worth. You don't need to show up everywhere. Constant availability often looks like desperation. And in your personal life, too, when you say no to marriage, children, parties, or traditions, people judge you.

They want you in their group, and when you refuse, they mock or abandon you. Please take your time before responding. Don't rush to say yes just because others do. One yes leads to ten more demands. Always remember: no means no. Prioritize yourself.

The Conditioning. That Made You Say Yes As children, we were trained to say yes.

"Say hello to Aunty."

"Show your dance."

"Sing in front of them." Refusing was not allowed.

Yes, was polite. No disrespect. That is where the habit of self-abandonment begins. So, when adults say, "I just can't say no," it is not cute. It is conditioning.

Loki's Story: A Life Derailed by Yes Loki's wealthy father wanted him to marry a girl for business ties. Loki wasn't ready. He loved someone else. But his parent's guilt-tripped him. "We sacrificed everything for you."

"Don't disappoint us."

"This is what is best for our family." He gave in. He said yes out of obligation, not love. Marriage came. A child came. But inside, he was collapsing. Years later, he met the girl he truly loved. A secret affair began. Eventually, the marriage broke. His child suffered the most. The lesson is simple.

Saying yes out of guilt can destroy the life you actually want. Loki's parents were the selfish ones. They manipulated him and left him broken. Prioritizing your well-being is never selfish.

Diana's Story: The Cost of Trying to Belong Diana moved from a small town to a metro city. Her new friends were rich, stylish, and confident. To belong, she said yes to everything: dinners, trips, and shopping. She couldn't afford it. She compromised her principles by doing unethical work just to blend in. Friend: "You're coming this weekend, right?"

Diana, forcing a smile: "Yeah, sure." Inside she was breaking. She didn't have the confidence or the money. But she wanted to belong so badly that she lost herself. The lesson is clear.

Be so sure of who you are, so rooted in your real qualities, that you never need to hide behind a fake image. No one can make you feel small unless you hand them that power yourself. Say no when you need to. Say yes only when it aligns with your values, dignity, and truth. The people meant for you will never demand that you lose yourself.

No, it isn't rejection. It is clarity.

Saying no does not make you rude, unkind, or arrogant. It simply means you are clear about your boundaries. But people misunderstand this, especially in love. A simple no becomes an ego wound. Rejection feels personal. It isn't personal.

It is clarity. It is easy to say yes just to avoid conflict, but it takes real strength to say no with honesty. When you say no, you are not rejecting someone. You are respecting yourself. And if someone cannot handle your refusal, it reveals their emotional fragility, not your flaw. Be like a mountain: firm, grounded, and unshaken. Say no to anything that disturbs your peace or values. Say it softly, but mean it. Protecting your energy is not selfish. It is self-respect.

Mindset Notes...

1. Find out who respects your refusal and who is offended. Notice the difference. It shows who truly values you.

2. Write down the things you did only out of pressure. Then list what you will never do again, and stand firm with it.

3. Observe your feelings whenever you say yes or no. Are you agreeing in peace or out of fear?

4. Do not fear solitude. Sometimes declining an invitation means walking alone for a while. That is better than being surrounded by people who drain your energy.

Part IV The Three Powers...

The Power of Communication, Networking, and Marketing

"Skills pave the way, but your network determines the rooms you're invited into."

The world is big, intriguing, and challenging. To succeed, you need courage, discipline, and resilience. But above all, there's one skill schools never taught us: the importance of communication, networking, and marketing. If no one recognizes your skills, someone less skilled will replace you, regardless of your intelligence. Skills alone are not enough; your ability to express yourself, connect, and influence will determine your path.

When we are in school, parents and teachers push us to catch up on the syllabus. They seldom teach us how to communicate effectively or build relationship skills that truly determine your opportunities in the real world.

Some people seem lazy or inefficient yet get ahead. Why? The answer is because they have mastered the art of persuading others of their capabilities. Whether they possess true skills or not is a matter for later; first, they successfully negotiate and secure the chance to demonstrate their abilities.

Communication and networking anchor you at every phase of life. If you can articulate your thoughts clearly, communicate effectively, and establish connections with the right individuals, you've already made significant progress. The rest is just persistence. Without communication, your life's purpose is incomplete.

Tone, Clarity, and Presence

People often misinterpret much of your life due to the tone you use. Others may dismiss you, not because of a lack of capability, but because your tone conveys authority when you are actually still learning.

Key elements for lasting communication:

1. Clarity**:** Speak with precision. Make sure others understand what you need, offer, or provide. Clear your inhibitions and practice confident speech.

2. The Power of Dressing: Your attire adds meaning to your communication. Dress appropriately for the occasion: office, shrine, meeting, or casual outing. Polished, comfortable footwear enhances confidence and creates a strong first impression. People often trust those who are organized in appearance because they assume they are organized in work too.

3. Misconceptions About Branded Clothing: Don't wear brands just to impress. Dress humbly for the milestone you've reached, not the one you hope to achieve. Overdressing can create unintended tension, especially with authority figures.

Practical Exercises for Communication:

. Spend 10 minutes daily practicing your tone by recording yourself and listening.

. Start one conversation per day with someone you disagree with to practice listening and understanding.

. Write one short gratitude note or message to a friend/family member daily to strengthen personal communication.

"Communication is invisible energy—more about listening than talking."

Communication in Your Personal Life

Communication is the foundation of harmony in personal relationships. To connect with family, partners, children, and friends, your words must reach the heart. Often, we feel misunderstood and stop communicating. Families fail to talk because everyone wants to be right. True communication is listening first, processing, and then understanding.

We communicate in more ways than speaking:

. Through deep listening

. Through silence

. Through our eyes

. Through poems, songs, and letters

. Through how we dress or show up

The main reason most people fail? They don't listen.

Communication—What I Really Learned

I think what I've understood about communication is this: it's a tool that must be encouraged inside the family first. I was fortunate to grow up in a house where I could question things. But there are so many homes where children are silenced the moment, they ask anything.

And I genuinely believe that asking questions, debating with your children, and even having arguments sometimes can open a person up. That's the only way a child grows into an adult who knows how to set boundaries. Being blunt and straightforward is beneficial, but knowing where to apply it is what matters.

Communication isn't just about talking. It's about speaking at the right place, with the right tone, to the right person. There will always be people who are offended, and that's fine. But you also need to know the art of melting things down, softening the edges, and still getting your message across. I've seen people crack a deal in one meeting or one phone call simply because they knew how to communicate.

I remember my sales days—making hundreds of calls in a day. After speaking to so many people, I realized something important: I only remembered two categories of personalities. There were those who spoke harshly, making you feel small, and those who spoke gently, making you feel valued.

Even when those gentle ones refused politely, you still felt impressed by them. The mediocre ones were forgettable. Over time, I realized people respond more to calm, clear, emotionally intelligent communication. Everything you want to say depends on your tone and your politeness.

People don't remember you for how you look. They remember how you made them feel, how well you listened, how you didn't judge, and how you spoke politely. Communication is the most important tool you can ever master.

It builds lifelong relationships, goodwill, and strong professional bonds. Now think about that one person in your life who blew your mind not because of their accent or their vocabulary, but because of their conviction when they spoke. That's the power of true communication.

Networking: Building Your Circle

If communication is your mother, networking is your father—that's precisely what my father taught me. Even capable people fail to maintain connections. Often, hesitation or fear of judgment holds us back. Let me tell you something: most people aren't thinking about you 24/7. Only those with extra time or drifting energy will have opinions about everything. In today's world, street-smart people often succeed over the privileged or educated.

Networking strengthens bonds professionally and personally, whether in seminars, meetups, online communities, or international conferences. I learned this myself. Despite knowing the importance of networking, I hesitated to approach people first, fearing it would hurt my ego. I also struggled with self-marketing. I thought talking about myself would seem boastful, so I kept it brief.

That changed when a friend approached me at a gathering, confidently introducing himself and sharing his skills without being pushy. He told me, "People have short memories. You have to be seen and remembered." That moment taught me the real meaning of communication, networking, and marketing: to be heard and remembered.

Today, he is not only my colleague but also my friend and mentor. Networking is a reciprocal process. It's about exchanging ideas and building bonds that last, not just collecting contacts. You don't need perfect grammar, polished speech, or boastfulness; you need authenticity and constructive energy. Show up; that's where you will meet people who are alike.

Communication Starts at Home

Your network determines the rooms you are invited into, not your skills. This chapter isn't about the technical details of communication. It's about the tiny shifts you make in your mindset every day. Everything starts from home. That's where you learn to talk, express yourself, and approach others.

. Talk to people.

. Talk about your interests.

. Don't hesitate.

. Make friends.

. Don't communicate to impress; communicate to learn. That's where real growth begins.

Pick up books that teach you communication strategies. Trust me, that's one investment that will help you more deeply than you realize.

Communication is not a show; it's a lifelong skill that silently carries you into better relationships, better opportunities, and better rooms.

Mindset Notes...

1. Communication and networking are not optional; they are survival tools. They determine how people perceive you, how much trust you earn, and how far you'll go.

2. Listen more than you speak.

3. Dress and present yourself thoughtfully.

4. Communicate in words and actions.

5. Build a network intentionally, online and offline.

6. Use social media wisely to reach and influence people.

7. Speak positively, elevate others, and practice gratitude.

Today, speak clearly, listen deeply, and connect genuinely. Build your network with authenticity and intention. Attend events, invest in relationships, and remember: communication is more than talking—it's an energy that creates trust, influence, and opportunity. The rooms you're invited into tomorrow depend on how present and authentic you are today.

THE MOST IMPORTANT ENERGY—MONEY

"Today, the world communicates in a new language.

This new language lacks a voice, yet it holds greater significance than any living entity.

This new tongue is the language of money."

What Is Money, and Why Is It Important?

According to my experience so far, money is nothing but energy. It lifts your confidence, provides self-assurance, and brings positivity into your life. With this energy beside you, people take your words and your presence more seriously. Without it, people question your intelligence, your skills, and sometimes even your personal integrity.

When you have big goals but lack financial resources, you may feel stuck and suffocated. You may have hundreds of ideas, but you can't execute them wisely. Frustration follows. Mental health suffers. When your financial resources are low and your needs are high, your confidence drops. An unstable bank balance sends anxiety soaring; your mind fogs, and creativity blocks. Why?

Because your basic needs aren't met. You haven't started saving or investing. You hold liabilities, not assets. Opportunities don't knock when survival itself feels uncertain.

The Real Reason Behind Your Relationship with Money

Your relationship with money didn't start today. It started in your childhood.

. Some of us saw our parents fight over money.

. Some watched them work day and night just to keep the house running.

. Some sacrificed their dreams so their siblings could study.

. Some people become anxious while spending.

. Some are scared of losing money.

. Some overspend to escape emotions.

. Some save obsessively.

. Some feel guilty buying even small things for themselves.

For many, money was not just currency. It was stress, fear, silence, or survival. And this is how our money personality gets formed. Childhood shapes your money mindset more than any school textbook ever did.

The Era of Comparison—The Silent Financial Killer

Another challenge today is constant comparison. Earlier, people compared themselves with neighbors. Today, we compare ourselves with billionaires on social media.

Here's the truth no one admits

The day you start comparing yourself with a king, you begin to feel like a pauper—empty, insecure, and helpless. The urgency to show your lifestyle as better than someone else's is a profit for brands...

but a debt for you. You can't afford the branded bag, yet you buy it on EMI.

You book trips you can't pay off, just to impress people who won't remember it tomorrow. You are living a life on rent, building an identity on borrowed money. Why are you making one purchase after another? For whom? This is not the life you want. This is the life you are pressured to live.

My Personal Experience

Like many, I believed saving was the most important thing. But when saving becomes the only goal, you sacrifice the most precious years of your life. Instead, enhance your financial knowledge and invest, even small amounts, in places where your money grows.

Here is the truth

In chasing numbers, we often miss life. I missed traveling, going out with friends, and enjoying experiences. We assume we have time. "I will earn now and live later." But time is limited. Money cannot be held tight forever. One day, you might look back and wish you had lived more while earning.

That balance, living and earning simultaneously, creates a fulfilling life. Never attach your happiness to money. Happiness is not determined by the amount of money in your bank account. It comes from within. Whether you have little or more, stay content, aware, and grateful. Enjoy life. Spend time with loved ones. Travel. Shop. Make memories. But never take your life or experiences for granted.

Why Money Is So Important

From birth to your last rites—food, shelter, education, medicine, entertainment, even death—everything requires money. This isn't materialism. It is survival. Independence teaches you the value of every rupee or dollar. Even those living with family feel financial pressure. Sharing a roof may lower rent but often raises emotional costs, sometimes even the price of peace.

Some live under their parents' shadow with predictable pocket money and lifestyle. But that doesn't cure the emptiness inside, the desire to build something of your own. Nature gave us everything for free: air, water, and land. Humans turned them into commodities, creating an endless loop of desire. One fulfilled wish led to the next. Are we acting out of need or greed?

Where the Problem Begins

The root problem starts in childhood. Money management was never taught. Schools taught algebra, not taxes. Schools taught geometry, not interest.

We were prepared to become employees, not financially independent thinkers. By the time we wake up, we are clueless about investing, multiplying money, or managing it wisely.

We confuse emotions with finances and then wonder why we struggle. Financial literacy is survival literacy. Reading and writing won't save you if you don't know how to earn, invest, and stand on your feet. Talking about money was taboo. People think wanting money is greed.

But earning ethically, building a life, and paying for your dreams is not greed. It is growth.

Wants, Needs, and Greed

Needs are urgency's foundation. Wants are desires, the extras. Greed is bottomless, the ego-driven hunger. Take Nancy. She comes from a decent family. Her parents work diligently and own their home. But Nancy wants independence, so she builds her legacy without borrowing. That's not greed. That's dignity.

Now compare such behaviours with those who chase a fake lifestyle through unethical means, bribery, scams, and smuggling. That is greed. Need pushes you to survive. Want pushes you to grow. Greed destroys both you and society.

Privilege vs. Underprivilege

When someone devastated by poverty works any job to survive, that is a necessity.

When someone securely chooses unethical shortcuts, that is greed. Globally, financial stress is everywhere: U.S. students are drowning in debt. Europe is facing housing crises. Australia's gig workers are struggling. Inflation reshapes survival worldwide. Money pressure is universal.

Key Myths vs. Truths Myth:

Myth: Money is evil.

Truth: Ignorance about money is evil.

Myth: Only the rich become richer.

Truth: Financial literacy can make anyone richer.

Myth: Discussing money is greedy.

Truth: Avoiding money talk keeps you poor.

Modern Financial Advice

We live in a digital era. Freelancing, YouTube, digital products, REITs, and opportunities are endless. Use your device to earn, not just scroll. Start vlogging, writing, or selling digital products, whatever suits your skills. But be cautious. Scams exist.

I once paid 200 dollars for a book marketing campaign, and the person vanished. Lesson: Use trusted platforms. AI is changing everything. Jobs will disappear. New ones will rise. Degrees won't guarantee survival. Skills will.

Smart Allocation:

. 40 percent savings

. 30 percent investment
. 15 percent insurance
. 15 percent lifestyle Grow slightly each year.
. Celebrate progress.
. Stagnancy kills motivation.

Money Equals Self-Respect

If you borrow money and delay delivering it on time, it can lead to a breakdown in trust. Trust collapses. Remember money is an exchange, but self-respect is forever.

Money Equals Relationship

Your relationship with money matters more than how much you earn. I have seen people sulk after spending on things they love.

I have observed that some people who have little money spend it lavishly, and as a result, money seems to flow toward them effortlessly. I have been both. After reading about manifesting abundance, I shifted my mindset.

Now I spend happily and confidently, knowing money will return multiplied. To earn money, you don't need a degree. You need awareness, discipline, and street-smartness.

Here is what no one teaches

Your relationship with people affects your money.

Arguments block opportunities. Goodwill opens opportunities. In the world of money, Remember, no one is your friend or your enemy. Everyone is a well-wisher only when you have something of value to offer. This statement is harsh yet accurate.

Financial Mistakes to Avoid:

. Buying Show-Off Items on EMI

. Relying on one income source

. Ignoring your credit score

. Skipping insurance

. Falling for quick-money traps

. Not learning digital skills

Final Thoughts

. Money buys options, not happiness.

. Money provides freedom, not identity.

Ask yourself: What is my relationship with money?

. Am I multiplying or just earning?

. Am I financially independent or emotionally dependent?

What mistake taught me the harshest lesson? Being broke is romanticized, but behind the scenes, it is anxiety, overthinking, and silent suffering.

Money provides you choices: the choice to walk away, to rebuild, to live on your terms. If you want freedom, master the world's most important energy, money. Money Is a Mindset You are not broke or wealthy. You carry a mindset that attracts or repels money. Believe you have enough, and you act that way.

Think you are broke, and you limit yourself. Money doesn't start in your wallet. It starts in your mind.

Mindset Notes...

1. **Assess Your Energy**—When you spend money, are you scared or fulfilled? Track your emotions for a week.

2. **Investment List**—List your top three preferred investment sources.

3. **Skill Mapping** – Write down skills you can add to earn money online or through social media.

4. **To-Do & Deadline**- Create a money-related task list. Even one ticked box is progress.

5. **Fear & Change**—Write your primary fear around money and what changes you want to implement.

6. Reflection on Needs vs. Wants vs. Greed For one week, **track a purchase or investment:** was it a need, a want, or driven by greed?

7. **Digital Income Plan** – Identify one online platform or tool you will start using this month to generate extra income.

As we discovered in this chapter, money holds powerful energy; it has become the source of almost everything. Money is essential to survive, but to truly thrive, we need people. And here lies the hidden danger: some people in our lives can create a toxic loop.

Dependency is that loop, whether emotional or financial, where you become stuck in constant need. It's a trap that sucks your confidence, blocks your growth, and slowly takes away your power. Next, we'll explore this dependency trap and how to escape it.

THE TRAP OF DEPENDENCY

"Attachment is unhealthy. Stop mistaking it for loyalty."

We meet people in our daily lives. We talk; we share our stories, our pain, and our routines. Some become close friends. Some become our emotional anchors. And through all my encounters, I realized one brutal truth: a major source of unhappiness is the inability to detach from people who constantly disturb your peace.

Many people discover themselves entangled with unsuitable parents, siblings, friends, partners, or workplaces. They remain in these situations not because they enjoy suffering, but because they lack the courage to detach... or they overthink the consequences more than their own emotional condition. This is the conditioning society has built in us:

"Family is everything."

"Blood is thicker than water."

"Stick together no matter what."

This maxim holds even when dealing with a toxic family member.

This applies even when a friend manipulates your self-esteem.

This concept holds even when your partner causes you trauma. This concept remains valid even if your job consumes your life. In relationships, people stay for years, tolerating emotional or physical abuse, because the trauma becomes familiar.

Detaching feels scarier than leaving. In friendships, there is always that one dominating personality pulling everyone's strings, while others stay because "we're old buddies." This is the normal state of many people's minds:

"It's okay."

"He's, my spouse."

"She's, my sister."

"We've known each other for years."

"At least we're together." But every small disrespect, every emotional hit, every manipulation piles up. And one day, you realize how weak and helpless you have become. People either break this pattern... or they pass it on. Like mother-in-law trauma—whatever she tolerated, she repeats with the next generation. This vicious circle is nothing but the trap of attachment. She develops an attachment to the places she visits. People are the objects of attachment There is a strong bond with memories.

There is also a strong connection to routines. Attachment leads to conflict and emotional destruction. Never confuse loyalty with attachment. Loyalty is a quality. Attachment is a mindset.

I remember a friend whose husband abused her—physically and emotionally. She mistook it as part of "love." She was taught since childhood that a husband shows both anger and care. It may sound strange in this modern era, but mindsets haven't evolved. Clothes are modern; thinking is still orthodox.

Another friend of mine is a single mother. Her family mistreats her. They speak rudely and never support her, but when they need something, she is the first person they call. Imagine knowing your family is exploiting you and still showing up out of duty. Thankfully, she broke the pattern.

Now she only visits them during genuine crises. She learned what many people still ignore: your peace is your responsibility. No one will think of you the way you must think of yourself. I know a male friend, divorced, still living with his parents, never moved out, and never became independent.

His mother is emotionally obsessed. She serves him everything—food, water, and clothes. She keeps him dependent because she fears loneliness. And now he is emotionally weak, unprepared for life, and trapped in comfort. You can guess why the marriage didn't survive. Why are people so attached even when it feels wrong? The fear of loneliness plays a significant role. This behaviour is primarily due to feelings of guilt.

This fear is primarily due to the conditioning that was instilled during childhood. Because they mistake attachment for loyalty. Because endurance becomes a habit. How do you break it? Awareness. Knowing that you are attached to the wrong person is a blessing. Once awareness enters, detachment becomes inevitable.

. Stop explaining yourself.

. Stop expecting explanations.

. Take distance like medicine.

The Pull of Power

Dependency doesn't only come from relationships. It comes from positions of power, too. Often, we meet people in positions of influence and feel drawn to them—not because we want to serve them, but because somewhere inside, we hope that proximity will provide us opportunities.

We think:

"If I stay close enough, loyal enough, helpful enough... maybe I'll acquire even half of what they have." But here's the truth:

When you walk on someone else's path, you don't receive what you earn. You only receive what's left over. In India, young people from small towns often fall into this trap. They spend their most energetic years running errands for influential people, getting ₹500 for rally participation not because they believe in the cause, but because they hope someone will notice them.

You can't shortcut your way into greatness by climbing on someone else's ambition. People will utilize you far more than they will uplift you. In your early years, you're naive, inexperienced, and searching for opportunities. That's when illusions become dangerous.

You hear lines like

"I'll call you."

"There's an interview coming."

"I'll introduce you to someone big." You believe them not because they're trustworthy, but because you've stopped believing in yourself. The real trap is not the promise—It is your doubt.

The fear that you can't move ahead without someone else's pull. In workplaces, such doubt shows up too. Some people guide you genuinely. Others deliberately share limited knowledge because they fear you will go ahead in life. Some want you dependent on them so you never grow beyond them. They provide you the fish every day but never teach you how to catch it. Take support and guidance, but don't let them become dependent. It blocks your growth.

This lesson is based on my personal experience

I also remember this from my own life, when I was working as a live host. There was a friend whom I genuinely believed to be trustworthy. For a long time, I believed he genuinely wanted the best for me—until I experienced a realization: I was never receiving the bigger opportunities. And it wasn't because I lacked talent. I was honest, ethical, hardworking, and consistent.

But he wasn't giving me the chances he gave others. One day, the truth slipped out.

He wasn't providing opportunities because I wasn't reciprocating the same "energy" he had for me. He said he wanted to marry me. I kept the relationship strictly work-related and respectful. But the moment he realized I wasn't giving him what he wanted emotionally, my career suddenly slowed down.

That day, I said something that changed everything inside me: "When I started, I started alone. With God by my side, no one can ever take away my opportunities. I was stern. I was hopeful.

And I was done depending on anyone's Favor. Later, I often wondered about other girls in similar situations—girls who doubt themselves, fear working lengthy hours, feel manipulated, or compromise because they have responsibilities and financial pressures.

Without judging anyone, I'll say this:

. People will point out your weaknesses

. They'll be critical.

. They won't acknowledge your effort.

. They'll act as if they are doing you a favor.

However, a strong mindset involves understanding this:

. You started alone.

. You will rise alone.

And the right opportunities will always reach you through the right people. Decent, ethical humans exist. You just need to believe in your ability.

The Illusion of Opportunity

I also remember a male friend who wanted a job in the Gulf. He waited for over nine months because someone had promised him a job placement in Kuwait. He invested lakhs of rupees, only to realize it was all an illusion. The man spoke confidently, acted trustworthy, and lured him with false hope. My friend was overly dependent on him, and he was robbed. Dependency doesn't always look emotional. Occasionally, it looks like waiting for an opportunity that was never real.

What Hurts the Most

The biggest pain when you are young and naïve isn't failure. It's wasted time.

. Time spent trusting the wrong people.

. Time spent believing empty promises instead of believing yourself.

. Time spent searching for shortcuts instead of building your own path.

You're not behind because you're not smart. You're behind because you were too kind, too trusting, and too low on self-belief. Depending on others delays your growth, your decisions, and your confidence.

Everyone in their early years of struggles has a vulnerable side. You trust easily. You don't yet know who is real and who is performing. Occasionally, someone says: "I'll crack this deal for you."

"I'll set your life straight." And when you're emotionally worn out, you believe them. If you're lucky, you meet a true mentor.

You lose something far more costly than trust if you don't—your time. This chapter may have discussed many forms of human emotions: dependency, attachment, detachment, illusion, and the people who drain you. But it's equally important to know this: all kinds of people exist in this world, and humanity is still functioning because of them.

Not all humans will drain you.

Some individuals will support you in unexpected ways. After everything you've read about attachment, influence, manipulation, dependency, and illusion, it's important to remember this truth: not every connection in life weakens you. Some relationships become your strength long after a person is gone.

Some people appear exactly when your world is collapsing, and they hold you up without expecting anything in return. And that is where goodwill comes in. Let me tell you a story that proves this.

The Story of Karan

Karan was in college when he got a sudden call from his mother asking him to come home immediately. No explanation. When he arrived, he learned the heartbreaking news—his father had passed away overnight due to a stroke. A month later, his father's assistant informed them about the company's financial troubles.

Karan's mother suggested pawning jewellery for household expenses, but Karan and the assistant refused. The assistant advised Karan to reach out to his father's old friends. He called one of them. The man promised to return by evening. By sunset, the doorbell rang.

Karan opened the door and saw five to six men standing with his father's friend.

These were the people his father had helped at different points in life.

Now they had returned to support his family when they needed it most. That day, Karan realized the real wealth his father had built. Not money. Goodwill. People remembered his father's kindness, generosity, and loyalty. Karan decided to carry his father's legacy forward. He valued people over profits and relationships over

shortcuts. Today, he has expanded the logistics business globally, proving that when you invest in people, the universe invests back in you.

The Next-Gen Dependency

With so much already said, here's what I think the current and next generations are stuck with. Parents provide shelter, comfort, and all basic needs for this generation. And for that reason, many of them believe they already have everything. They feel they have limited things to achieve.

Their basic survival needs are met, which leads to confusion about their ambitions. One day, they see someone's post and feel inspired. The next day, they watch Shark Tank and dream of becoming entrepreneurs. Then a reel goes viral, and they follow that trend too. A motivational speaker shouts online, and for a moment, they feel charged. But it fades in twenty-four hours. This generation is not innocent.

. They are naïve.

. They believe too easily.

. They absorb too quickly.

They are influenced before they even understand what influenced them. Therapy has now become a trend. Some individuals attend therapy simply because their friends are participating. Healing has become a fashion, not a process. For many, therapy is a display board, not a transformation.

Following fashion and trends is convenient. Looking rich and actually being rich have become two different lifestyles. Everyone wants to "make money doing nothing," because a reel said it's possible. Being an atheist is considered cool. Extramarital affairs are normalized as "my life, my wish."

As noted earlier, media and social media have a profound impact on our culture. Unlike older generations, the next generation will not rely on parents or partners.

They will be dependent on infotainment. Noise will replace their wisdom. Algorithms shape their choices. Their lifestyle, career, personality, and relationships—believe it or not—will be influenced by what they consume. Distraction has emerged as the latest form of dependency.

Screen addiction is the new emotional attachment.

And the dangerous part is this:

They won't even realize they're becoming dependent, because everything they depend on will feel convenient.

Then there is AI.

AI was designed to assist you. But if you are not aware, you will become dependent on it too. AI will think faster, respond faster, and create faster—and slowly, the human mind will become lazy, weak, and comfort-addicted. But remember this:

Humans were created to make.

. To explore.
. To innovate.
. To think.

To imagine without limits. You are meant to lead your thoughts, not borrow them.

You are meant to navigate your journey, not outsource it to trends. You are meant to live with awareness, not distraction. If this generation does not learn to detach from constant exposure, the next generation will lose the ability to think independently. And that is the real danger. Life becomes lighter the day you choose yourself, even when no one chooses you back.

Mindset Notes...

1. Write down the names of the people you call for every random thing, the ones without whom you feel you can't function.

2. Identify the people who push you to take risks, think bigger, and grow.

3. Write down your fears—the ones that stop you from moving forward. Seek knowledge.

4. Pick at least three skills, subjects, or current trends to learn this month.

Part V
Escape, Purpose & Higher Ground...

Temporary Highs and Permanent Disconnection

"Every high that lights you up also carry the power to dim you—and those lost years never return".

Let's be honest: drugs, alcohol, and porn have become the modern painkillers for depression, anxiety, loneliness, rejection... even celebration.

If your father owns $100 billion and you're in your mid-20s, still wondering how to start while you party every night in clubs or house gatherings with booze, illicit drugs, and sex, and if you've become casual about it yet have enough money to check into rehab, come back sober, maybe join your father's business later, or use his network to build something.

Then let's be real: you've wasted your years, but without any real loss. In your heart, you understand that all you are is your father's shadow. People socialize with you and take you seriously not because of who you are, but because of him. You throw lines like, "Do you even know who my father is?" And for a second, you feel superior. But inside?

You know the truth. You know how suppressed you are. I'm not here to offend anyone. I'm speaking directly to those who are independent, the ones trying to build something on their own. You've got a spark. You want to build your own name. And for that, you've got to protect your mind like it's your last shield. Because in this world, there are things designed to destroy you.

Things everyone knows are harmful, yet they're still sold, glamorized, and used to manipulate the most vulnerable. They've targeted you since school. Parents, teachers, and society—they all warned you.

You know what drugs do. You know what porn does. Yet there's still a world telling you it's no big deal. One puff, one pill, one video—it's harmless. Normal. Chill. And that's precisely how you fall.

When the Trap Looks Like a Party

Yes, I'm talking about drugs. We all know we shouldn't go near them. Still, people try just a harmless puff, just one line to feel alive. That one-time thrill can destroy not just you, but a whole generation. In your most colorful, exciting years, parties, festivals, friends, and music tempt you. Peer pressure pulls you. The media promotes it as if it's a tasty treat. Movies, music videos, and influencers—they show people using marijuana, cocaine, and pills like they're living the dream.

Here's the truth:

Someone else's tragedy might look like comedy to you... until it becomes yours.

And it's happening everywhere from Mumbai to Madrid, New York to Nairobi. In cities like L.A. and London, the situation is heartbreaking. Many don't even have a home to return to. They sleep on the streets. For them, chasing a hit is easier than chasing dreams. Teens in schools have easier access to substances than ever in history.

What looks like harmless "fun" becomes dependency, stealing years, talent, and potential. Consider whether this "therapy" truly provides relief or if you're simply another client funding someone else's empire.

As I discussed in my habit chapter, routine may seem boring. But instead of taking a pill, why not go running? Feeling overwhelmed? Journal. Share your heaviest thoughts with a trusted friend. No matter how appealing it looks, don't walk through that door.

Anyone who left home for these places has either never come back or has lost precious years. You must master the business of self-control. I've seen it up close. My wealthy, well-to-do cousin drowned in cocaine. It made him aggressive, moody, and unstable. Rehab became his second home. He'd be released, then chase the same drugs again. Today, he's still there watching the best years of his life dissolve into white powder.

Remember this:

Do something once or twice, and it becomes a habit. Everyone else moves away, and only your family suffers. That is the highest price you will pay. Start small. Delete the app constantly demanding your attention. Walk daily, even for ten or thirty minutes. Keep journaling. Be friends with a book and a pen. Pour yourself out there instead of pouring yourself into illusions.

The Performance Trap

Drugs aren't just taken to chill. Many take them to perform. Rappers, singers, and actors glamorize drug use as a lifestyle. I once met a theatre artist who admitted he couldn't step on stage without smoking weed—it calmed his nerves. We've heard of athletes taking pills or powders to boost focus and stamina.

Countries like Kenya, Pakistan, and Afghanistan—major suppliers—thrive off this trade, while the greed of a few destroys the lives of many. Alcohol is no different. Alcohol has become a normal part of celebrations, relationships, and culture. While you feel like being high, people around you often suffer. Parents battle alcohol or drugs, ruining childhoods.

Marriages collapse. Crimes occur. Lives are wasted. Substances don't just numb; they control you. They dictate your mood, choices, relationships, and future. Some use them to "destress." At best, they help once or twice. But life isn't meant to be escaped; it's meant to be lived. Every time you turn to a substance instead of your strength, you're proving weakness, not resilience. There is only one story, one life.

Ten Years Lost

Let me tell you about a friend. He grew up in a broken home with criticism every day and no emotional support. As a teen, he smoked pot. Then came alcohol. Subsequently, he began to experiment with stronger drugs. Somehow, he completed engineering. But once college ended, he fell straight back into the cycle.

Every relationship failed. He blamed the women, calling them selfish and disloyal. Years later, after undergoing therapy, he admitted the truth: it was his behaviour that caused the failures. It was him. He judged his parents, held onto anger, and used destruction as self-punishment. He didn't want to survive; he wanted to disappear.

Now he's in his 50s. Alone. He is currently traveling around the world. He remains ill-prepared for a romantic relationship.

. The damage runs deep.

. Healing takes time.

. Sometimes time isn't enough.

And he's not alone. I met a young woman, a dancer, vibrant and romantic—who lost everything to cocaine. Today, she's in rehab, learning to walk away from the one thing she thought gave her freedom. Addiction steals futures quietly, one dream at a time.

Porn—The Invisible Predator

Once sacred and intimate, sex is now a top global business. The porn industry exploded over the last three decades. Young people choose it as a career. But not everyone processes exposure the same way. For some, even a kissing scene triggers discomfort. For others, nudity becomes casual.

And porn? It's not just in bedrooms; it's in pockets, cafés, buses, and offices. People secretly watched it escape. And while they do, we hear of molestation, abuse, rape—even crimes against women, children, and animals. Who takes accountability? Nobody.

We punish individuals but rarely address the root. Not all addictions are chemical. Some are digitally silent but deadly. Porn creates unrealistic expectations, destroys relationships, and manipulates the vulnerable.

Desire becomes obsession. Obsession becomes addiction. Many porn actors face exploitation, mental illness, STDs, and HIV. The money-makers behind the industry don't care. Relationships collapse. Intimacy becomes numb. Emotional health deteriorates in ways science is still trying to measure.

No One Will Carry Your Baggage for You. Your mind. Your trauma. Your sadness. You can share it, but don't expect anyone to carry it for you. Your baggage is yours. Hold it too long, and it will break you. Nobody's coming to save you. You can stay stuck, repeating, "Life's not fair," or you can protect what's left of your peace—one choice at a time. Start small. Delete the addictive app. Walk daily. Journal. Befriend a book and pen. Express your real self instead of indulging illusions.

Choose the Real High.

- Are you seeking a chemical high? It won't last.

- The applause? It fades.
- The porn? Hollow.
- The drug? Soul-eating.

You want a real high?

- Build something.
- Show up for your people.
- Talk about your wounds instead of numbing them.
- Fall in love.
- Sit in silence.
- Go into nature.
- Listen to music.
- Forgive. Choose you.

When the noise subsides, it's just you. If you destroy yourself, nobody will mourn as deeply as you imagine. Choose wisely. You matter. Your mind is your last home. You receive only one body. One brain. One chance. Temporary highs fade—but the scars of disconnection last forever. Don't let your story become one of them.

Global Reality

Alcohol, drug, and porn addictions are among the most significant challenges of the modern world. They aren't "bad habits"—they're soft weapons aimed at youth.

Rehab canters are full of young people losing their best years. When they come out, half their life has slipped away. Those who use substances casually during work, study, or day-to-day life battle mood swings that wreck personal and professional lives.

Slowly, they lose the ability to separate illusion from reality.

And here's the cruelest part:

The suppliers, producers, and dealers keep their families far away from the poisons they sell to you. It's heartbreaking to see brilliant young people who could build, create, and shape the world succumb to these traps.

The high feels powerful in the moment. But it's the quickest way to hand your power to someone else. Those who chase temporary highs end up permanently lost. Some are building their bank balance while you're losing yourself—feeling numb, lost, addicted. Don't let their profit become your prison.

Mindset Notes...

If you're young and reading this:

1. Spend more days out with friends. Go into nature. Celebrate life.

2. Avoid watching unhealthy porn just to escape boredom or loneliness.

3. Learn to turn down parties that feel suspicious. If the vibe is wrong, trust that instinct.

4. If you know you have an addictive nature, be honest—say no to drugs and cut ties with anyone who pulls you toward them.

5. Fill your mind with better fuel. Watch content that teaches you. Listen to inspiring podcasts that influence you positively.

In this chapter, you confronted the harsh realities of the world and how pressure and frustration push people into destructive habits. Habits that come back to haunt individuals can have significant emotional and physical consequences, resulting in the loss of valuable years from their lives.

In the next chapter, we will explore the shields that will protect you when life throws challenges at you and how you can turn those challenges into learning, navigate your way, and live a healthy life.

The Shield is a Must-Have

"You were taught to chase, compete, and run, but no one taught you how to build your inner power, peace, and balance — the shield that protects you from chaos."

The days when life was solely defined by spirituality are over. The present day is a new era, one where you begin your life with it before stepping into the wild world. Use spirituality as your protective layer, not as an excuse to accept defeat. What Is Spirituality? People today are increasingly embracing modern living and often exhibit qualities of self-centeredness.

Many can manipulate situations to their advantage. Some innocent people, facing life's challenges, seek guidance from gurus or spiritual teachers who promise to illuminate their path. Spirituality is not God, religion, or immortality. It simply means elevating one's consciousness to a higher state of awareness. Being present is the essence of spirituality. Living in the present moment without constantly dwelling on the past or future saves you from guilt and anxiety.

Spirituality is accepting that humans make many mistakes, acknowledging them one by one, and learning from them instead of punishing yourself. Unfortunately, many organizations present themselves as "spiritual" while leading young people into destructive habits or even illegal activities. Some may charge a hefty amount to teach you methods that are inaccessible to everyone, which is why it's crucial to understand what spirituality truly is.

Here is why I recommend pursuing a spiritual path during your peak years.

Discovering spirituality early in life is a blessing. This isn't everyone's calling, but to be part of it or at least offer it a try is essential. When you are young, you will be inexperienced. Many of you might come from a background that is disoriented or unstable.

So many people are simply seeking peace, warmth, and affection from others. They want to place their expectations on someone else's shoulders. There is self-pity, lack of awareness, and missing guidance. If you seek guidance early, tell me, what is the harm? I believe knowing what you don't want is more important than knowing exactly what you do want. Spirituality provides you that power.

Effective habits require practice. You must align your mind, body, and emotions so life flows in a way that keeps you sane. Whatever you do for your sanity is for your benefit; it is not a favor to anyone else. I only want to guide you so you know yourself, who you are, and what you want. Life will never be smooth; it is uncertain by nature. But with self-awareness, life becomes clearer. Challenges will arise, solutions will present themselves, and you will stop living with a mindset that only complains. You will become accountable for your life.

My Vipassana Experience:

The Turning Point Allow me to share an experience I discovered in a phase of my life when I was restless, directionless, and manipulated in relationships, unaware and confused. This was in my mid-20s. I had a spiritual experience that shaped who I am today. It introduced me to qualities a human can embody: strength, resilience, and accountability.

One major shift was the disappearance of self-pity. I recognized it as one of the most damaging emotions a human can carry. It breaks bonds, blocks progress, and fuels blame, dependency, anxiety, and emotional instability.

I realized where I had been going wrong in life. I decided to experience my emotions fully and accept responsibility for my life and decisions, regardless of the challenges I faced. This shift

happened because I attended a Vipassana course, which I believe is one of the purest forms of meditation. The legendary Gautam Buddha, who attained enlightenment, practiced Vipassana, a thousand-year-old practice. Through this spiritual discipline, this meditation has been practiced by many generations.

They don't charge any fee but expect discipline, honesty, and adherence to the guidance for the 10-day course, offering light purely through the teachings of Buddha. Vipassana was life-changing. I remember every second, every word, every moment of silence, and the strange lightness I felt. I arrived feeling heavy and unclear, but I emerged feeling like an entirely new person. My problems didn't vanish; life's challenges actually grew. But my approach changed:

I reacted less, responded more, and practiced holding no grudges. The concept became firmly ingrained in my subconscious. It was a gradual transformation, not an instant one. For years after, I made it a point to attend the course every year.

Most importantly, I retained what I learned during the course. Until today, I hold tight to the teachings, and I ensure that I apply them. But if you think that after that I stopped arguing, stressing, or feeling anxious, you're wrong. These emotions very much stayed with me. The difference was that I now dealt with them with much more clarity than restlessness.

If you were born in India, the traditional roots your ancestors upheld are among your greatest blessings. Yoga, shared with the world, is one of these blessings. It eases life's challenges, reduces anxiety, and aligns body and mind.

Only the wisest beings understand that external achievements cannot replace the calm and clarity of sitting surrounded by nature, practicing yoga and meditation. Just like a warrior prepares before going to battle, we must prepare before stepping into life's challenges.

Spiritual practices serve as a crucial part of that preparation, acting as a shield. Humans tend to overthink, question, and become upset. It is highly recommended to jot down your feelings in a journal. Neuroscience shows that writing by hand directly connects to the brain, deepening intellect and emotional intelligence.

When you write your deepest feelings, you might feel a release; the heaviness disappears. Writing helps you forgive, let go, and preserve energy you would have spent confronting toxic people. It is not about seeking answers; it is about clearing your mind. A lighter mind manifests more clearly and accurately.

I hope the next time you feel weighed down, you write it down and share your experience.

Spirituality in Everyday Life

Spirituality has different meanings for everyone, but its essence is the same:

. Freedom from attachment

. Neutrality in happiness and sadness

. Deep self-awareness

There is magic in affirmation; it charges your subconscious to believe in life's possibilities.

. If you have a voice, speak eloquently or remain silent.

. If you have a mind, think positively or refrain from negative thoughts.

. If you have a body, nourish it or eat less to respect it.

With daily practice, emotions no longer sink deep into your core. Sadness or joy will still be felt, but they will remain at the surface instead of weighing you down.

Whether through meditation, yoga, or mindful living, you will feel charged. You don't need to force any specific practice; simply desire to live a life where your habits, emotional intelligence, and spiritual grounding protect you.

Stop blaming; start living. Humans experience mood swings and emotional highs and lows. Why?

Comparison: You may feel content, yet you are stuck comparing yourself to others. Embrace your uniqueness and respect the uniqueness of others.

Avoiding Truth: Sometimes the truth is right in front of you, but pride or ignorance makes you ignore it. This multiplies problems.

Redefining Success: Society defines success as education, a stable job, marriage, kids, and milestones. True success is living in the present, appreciating what you have, and making the most of it. It's okay to earn less, not travel, or not own a big house. True success is peace and love.

Healthy Attachment: Humans crave love, mentorship, and guidance. Technology has increased physical distance but intensified mental attachment through social media. People confuse self-love with selfishness.

Habits become addictions, and emotional dependency grows. Even a small step inward, exploring your inner world, reveals where your problems lie. Spirituality and conscious living help clear hurdles one by one.

The Power of Intuition

As a young, restless soul, one of the most important powers you need is intuition. It appears and disappears, sometimes quietly, sometimes loudly. Some follow it; some ignore it, overthinking the external environment. Later, they may regret not listening earlier. Intuition, if nurtured and followed, rarely leads you astray.

Many young people, busy following others, miss its power. I humbly acknowledge that I have made numerous mistakes. I didn't care to listen to my intuition. I completely avoided it, especially when choosing friends. I neglected a lot of uncalled-for behaviour from people in life.

While my inner gut refused, I kept giving them chances. Internally, a voice always said, "Not this time," but I ignored it. It is only now, while I am writing this book, that I realize that this phase taught me to be stern and reject the toxicity of people. If I learned such lessons in my 30s, imagine how difficult it is for those who are much younger and already trapped.

Therefore, don't wait until you're 30 to make decisions you should have made earlier. Occasionally, it is necessary to balance logic and emotion for your own mental comfort. Strengthen your intuition now.

In the coming days, humans will rely increasingly on technology, AI, automation, and gadgets. People will grow dependent. In that chaos, intuition will be your only compass. Use it to read people, sense situations, and navigate opportunities. It's not magic; it's your inner shield.

Mindset Notes...

1. Those who believe that money can solve all problems are unaware that even millionaires can lead chaotic lives. So yes, earn money, but prioritize peace above all else. Your goal should be to live in peace and love, accept yourself, and be fulfilled. Once you achieve that, you will see the positive in others.

2. If life feels challenging, don't devote extra attention to misery; it's normal. Locate solutions. Let spirituality enter your life. The sooner, the better.

3. Spirituality isn't an escape from life; it's a shield that lets you live fully. Begin now.

4. Understand that comparison ruins peace of mind. Move forward and recognize greater challenges like gender inequality. Don't chase perfection; it's a myth. Some days you will feel elevated, and some days you will locate yourself at the bottom

5. Nothing in life is constant; your habits will change, your perception will change, your friends will change, and your mindset will change. Whatever changes, acceptance is the answer. Take your time, but don't become lost.

6. Young blood must carry the wisdom that the challenge isn't men vs women; it's the mindset created centuries ago.

Mindset Questions for Self-Growth

1. What is the biggest mistake I'm still avoiding confronting, and why?

2. How often do I let fear of failure stop me from trying something meaningful?

3. Which past failure taught me the most—and did I truly learn from it?

4. Am I blaming others for failures that were actually mine to own?

5. Am I curating my life for approval or living it for myself?

6. How much time do I waste comparing myself to people I don't even know?

7. Does seeing someone else's success motivate me or make me feel less?

8. How often do I seek validation online instead of trusting my instincts?

9. Am I being authentic in my posts and conversations, or performing for approval?

10. Do I love people for who they are, or for how they make me feel about myself?

11. Am I afraid of being alone, and does that fear drive my relationship choices?

12. Which toxic relationships am I holding onto because I fear change?

13. How often do I communicate my real feelings instead of staying silent to avoid conflict?

14. Am I giving people what I expect from them, or expecting what I refuse to provide?

15. Am I financially literate enough to survive independently?

16. If I lost all my money tomorrow, how would I rebuild—and would I survive mentally?

17. Am I making money for freedom, growth, or just social validation?

18. How often do I spend impulsively, and what does that reveal about my emotional state?

19. Do I value experiences and knowledge over temporary material comforts?

20. Am I chasing a career or just a pay check?

21. What is my "real" work—the thing that provides me fulfilment beyond money or status?

22. Am I settling for comfort over challenge in my professional life?

23. Do I have the courage to pivot if my current path is not aligned with my purpose?

24. Am I learning skills that will make me future-proof, or just following trends?

25. Who am I when no one is watching?

26. How much of my personality is truly mine, and how much is shaped by society, friends, or family?

27. Which lies do I tell myself daily to feel safe or accepted?

28. Do I honour my values, even if it means facing criticism

29. Am I proud of the person I see in the mirror today?

30. What am I avoiding because it scares me, even if it's necessary for growth?

31. How often do I choose convenience over courage?

32. What would I attempt if I knew failure wasn't permanent?

33. Which relationships, jobs, or habits have I kept just because they are "comfortable"?

34. Am I ready to challenge societal expectations and carve my path?

35. How often do I ignore my gut because I fear judgment?

36. When was the last time I trusted intuition and it changed my life?

37. Am I listening to subtle signs in my body, mind, and environment?

38. Do I recognize opportunities that intuition signals, or dismiss them as coincidence?

39. How would my life change if I fully trusted myself?

40. Do I give myself permission to feel, or do I suppress emotions to appear strong?

41. How often do I let anger, jealousy, or resentment control me?

42. Am I seeking solutions, or just repeating the same negative thought loops?

43. Which emotional habits are quietly sabotaging my life?

44. How often do I check in with myself instead of getting lost in external chaos?

45. If I died tomorrow, what would I regret not doing?

46. How do I want to be remembered by friends, family, and the worlds?

47. Am I living to leave an impact, or am I just surviving day by day?

48. What would I change today if I truly valued the next ten year

49. Am I prepared to be accountable for my choices, no matter how uncomfortable?

Note: You don't need to write the answers down. Let these questions sit in your mind, make you pause, and challenge the way you view your life. Reflection is the first step toward transformation.

ACKNOWLEDGMENTS

To my dearest Goddess Saraswati, thank you for blessing me with the wisdom to write this book.

To my loving and respected father and grandfather — I miss you every day.

I feel the presence of my guiding angels and all the beautiful souls watching over me.

This life is magic, and I owe it all to you, Almighty.

I am deeply grateful to the universe.

May every reader who picks up this book receive love, light, and a little more clarity on their path.

Afterword

Dear Reader,

As you have reached this far and are reading it now, I want you to understand something clearly.

The purpose of this book is to remind you that human civilization has always been the same. All people, past, present, and future, feel the same emotions, reactions, and responses. We are many, yet only a few become exceptions. Their status is not due to their possession of material wealth or influence.

Instead, it is because they refused to follow the path that others had carved. They unlearned many things before learning new ones.

They accepted their defeats, their strengths, and their weaknesses. And you must know this. Everything you want is already within you. It is only the noise outside that blocks your mindset.

We were raised to blend in, to be one of all. As you learn about this world, you'll see how vital it is to set your own rules and priorities. Life is not a race where you must go beyond others. And even if it were, where is the finishing line?

The truth is that this race is nothing but a manipulation created by people who were distracted, who never conquered themselves, so they built conditioning and rules to control others: their likes, dislikes, dreams, and even their identity. All the while, they were living their lives freely. This book guides you toward the basics that bring out your uniqueness through habits, emotional intelligence, the power of saying no, understanding energies, and building a mindset that protects your peace.

With so much happening around you, your job is to maintain pace and balance.

Balance is the key. Have fun. Become distracted. Seek. Rest.

Do not rush. Take your time.

But always keep the key to your door.

Do not become lost.

Life is precious and beautiful, and it has a purpose. Your being here is purposeful.

Avoid wasting your time by being ordinary.

Take full advantage of your life.

Choose that one meaningful thing that makes you content and fulfilled. And most importantly, hold on to your uniqueness.

You were born special.

CONTACT THE AUTHOR

For updates, events, and new releases, follow:

Instagram: @connect.khushboo
X (Twitter): @KhushbooSh05
Facebook: /connect.khushboo
Website: thekhushboosharma.com
Email: connect.khushboosharma@gmail.com

KS

www.ingramcontent.com/pod-product-compliance
Lightning Source LLC
Chambersburg PA
CBHW050015170726
48282CB00025B/416